Conversations with the Water:
A Memoir of Cultivating Hope

By Michelle Linn-Gust, Ph.D.

CHELLEHEAD
WORKS

ISBN: 978-09723318-9-0
Library of Congress Control Number: 2011911619

Chellehead Works books are available at special discounts when purchased in bulk for premiums and sales promotions as well as fundraising and educational use. For details, contact the Special Sales Director at:
info@chelleheadworks.com
505-266-3134 (voice)
Albuquerque, New Mexico

Printed in the United States of America
First printing December 2012

Designed by Megan Mickey
Photography by Pamela Joye
Edited By Elizabeth Hadas

TABLE OF CONTENTS

ACKNOWLEDGEMENTS

I mostly kept this book under wraps while I was writing it, having found that the more I talk about I'm writing, the less I write (and so remain several unfinished manuscripts). Thank you to Sam and Lois Bloom for giving me their dining room table for two weeks in California and sending me off surfing in the morning and making sure I wrote the rest of the day (except when Sam bribed me to run errands with him by offering to take me to In-n-Out Burger for dinner). Thank you to Jill LaMorie for giving me the time to work on the book. Thank you to Mom who looked puzzled when for the first time I refused to tell her what I was writing. Thank you to Anne Cronin-Tyson who said this "sign post" needed to be written. Thank you to Wayne Barcheski and Ron Williams at SCORE who initially told me not to write this book and to Rita Riordan, also at SCORE, for setting them straight and seeing that this transition book did need to be written. Thank you to Sandy Keck for the feedback. Thank you to Beth Hadas for the quick turnaround. Thank you to Megan Mickey for putting together the cover over pie at Mannie's with me. Thank you to Pamela Joye for taking me in one weekend in September for the photo shoot on the East Coast and creating the essence of the book without knowing much about it.

*For anyone who walked any part of this road, even just a few steps, with me.
Somewhere the words you spoke to me are woven into this book.*

PROLOGUE

I worried this book would be too short. Time was getting away from me. I had a timeline to finish it, and life took over. Suddenly I was drowning in several projects that were coming to a head and finishing this book was looming.

Because it's my eighth book, there were many lessons from the past that I could draw from. I knew that somehow I would get it done, and I found myself constantly praying for help to finish it, to make it what it was supposed to be, but mostly to let go of what I couldn't control and just worry about finishing it.

It was then that I finally began to see I was trying to include too much. This book isn't the end of my writing. It's more the beginning, the start of a new road, a transition. There are many hints and threads throughout this book of what is to come next in my writing. I know the next two books I will write, and I am constantly jotting down thoughts about them on sticky notes because I know that first I must finish what is right in front of me.

Conversations with the Water: A Memoir of Cultivating Hope is not the story of my grief journey. I've written about that several times in previous books. Instead, what I write here is where I am today, how I got here, and what is most important to me as I go forward. I have written and spoken about grief backward, forward, inside out, and upside down. It's time for me to write about other inspiring topics as life takes me on a new road, one that starts where I have been before and moves me ahead to the person I am supposed to be.

INTRODUCTION

Astrology-minded people would say that I'm attracted to water because I'm a Sagittarian, a fire sign. That might be true, but the why doesn't matter much so much as what water does for me. I grew up wishing I had a swimming pool in the backyard. My sister Denise and I sometimes plotted how a pool could easily fit between two strategically placed rocks in our half-acre yard. We didn't care how far-fetched this was because our father, a depression baby, would never spend the money for a pool. He wouldn't even buy new pants, wearing stained and holey ones each day. Instead he left money behind without ever enjoying it.

Sometimes Dad would send away for travel brochures. Denise and I would pore over where we might get to stay in Myrtle Beach, South Carolina. We never did spend the night there, only stopping for about an hour on one trip. We dreamed of vacations at the beach. The happiest memories of my growing up years are those that revolve around water.

I didn't understand my connection to water. I just knew I loved it, that it inspired me. I can't even describe why but there is something about the way the sky reflects off it, the way it feels cool when I immerse myself in it, and the simple pleasure of being near it. When I had my own swimming pool, I drew as much strength from it as I did from the New Mexico sun. When Fred, the man with whom I coached track and cross-country, showed up one evening to tell me that one of our former athletes had killed himself, I withdrew to the pool after he left, swimming lap after lap, trying to understand why Justin would end his life.

One day, after my husband Joe and I had decided to end our marriage and that I would be the one to move to Chicago, where we had a second home, I stood by the swimming pool and thought about how easy it would be to stay. Yes, for the pool. I'd have given up a new car for the pool. I loved that pool. But I knew it was time to go on and I was going to have to work toward having a new pool, maybe a bigger pool, in my future. We couldn't stay together, and it wasn't worth staying over a 17,000-gallon concrete pond.

Surfing would replace the pool in many ways. I wouldn't see that at first but as the year progressed it became obvious. And in that time, I also saw how conversations with the water in my life helped me to be who I am. And where I am on this life journey. This is how I got there.

Part I

1

Surfing is life. The rest is details.

I loved that saying although it meant little in my life. Growing up in the Chicago suburbs I wrote it all over my school folders. My Barbies had plastic orange surfboards, but it wasn't something I ever thought I would get to do. I caught the surfing bug in junior high even though living in Chicago wasn't the only reason I wouldn't get to surf. It wasn't really something that girls did in the late 1980s. We only heard about boys surfing, not girls—except for Gidget, of course.

So even though I didn't think I'd ever do it because I didn't think I was coordinated enough (not realizing that my leg strength from years of running cross-country and track would be enough to balance me on the board) and because I didn't live near an ocean, I tore out pages from surfing magazines and taped them to my walls, giving them prized space next to all my Top 40 favorites like Bryan Adams. I bought board shorts and a turquoise Catch It surfing T-shirt, one that I wore with an oversized Forenza belt and an Esprit skirt. I bought the shirt on layaway at a boutique-like surf-clothing shop on a corner in my hometown in the Chicago suburb of Naperville. I paid for it with babysitting money.

"Surfer Girl" was not a nickname that I thought I would earn. "Pseudo Surfer Girl" might have been better for me. I developed an affection for surfing in junior high through my sudden obsession at thirteen to move to California (although I didn't quite make it that far, ending up in New Mexico for seventeen years instead).

But never in a million years did I really think I would get up on a board. People think I'm fearless. This is a misconception. I was not a good athlete in elementary school; I never could climb the rope in gym class. Heck, I couldn't even get up past where I started. I got picked next to last for every sport that involved a team. And when I started running in junior high, I threw up at starting lines, putting too much pressure on myself to do well. Sometimes life has a way of changing us, although sometimes I think I simply learned to hide my fear because I knew that if I didn't step out of the box I wouldn't experience new things. And it was through those experiences that I saw my growth and the fun I could have doing them. Running taught me to push myself and that I had no limits. Degrees were easy to get compared to many other life experiences. You followed the rules and did what they laid out for you to do. You didn't have to forge your own path; someone else did it for you. I loved speech class in high school and learned the lessons that would prepare me for public speaking (take your time, look directly at the people in the audience, write your speech in notes rather than sentences). I had been speaking in public for so many years by the time I got to my dissertation defense that it was easy to stand in front of my committee with my PowerPoint presentation behind me and talk about it.

But surfing? It was cool to watch. I didn't think I'd ever make it up on a board.

And then I went even farther away from California. Life would never be the same after my trip to Vermont and the long series of events that took me there.

2

I ended up in Vermont because I couldn't find a parking space.

Craving a burrito one day for lunch, I'd driven just two miles to my favorite restaurant in Albuquerque, the Frontier. After eating there for seventeen years, it was the first time I couldn't find a place to park. I drove around several times, baffled, finally paying to park, something I'd never done in all my years of Frontier dining.

My burrito stowed safely beside me in the car, I drove home in traffic as slow as molasses. New Mexico is truly the land of mañana. If you are in a hurry, don't go to New Mexico. For the first time in a very long while, I began to tell myself I needed a vacation. I loved and still love New Mexico but I needed a change of scenery. I had been traveling on and off for several years, but life was keeping me at home that summer working on a large web site. My only trip was to Tulsa, Oklahoma, to speak at a conference. I loved the people of Oklahoma, but it was July and would be 100 degrees. That wasn't a vacation.

I went down the list of friends whom I could visit, and whom I'd find fun and interesting to spend time with, and landed on one of my high school friends, Kim, and her husband, Rob. I hadn't seen them since my wedding, in 1999. They had since moved from Virginia to Vermont and had three kids, none of whom I'd ever met. It was time to go sample the maple syrup that Kim talked about and to meet Ella, the oldest, whom I'd made a quilt for.

What I didn't anticipate was Kim's joking suggestion that I take surfing lessons while I was there. We had planned to visit her sister Lisa, who had just moved to Rye, New Hampshire, on the coast.

"Yeah, right," I messaged back to her.

But the more I thought about it, the more I realized it wasn't so absurd. Why couldn't I try what I'd always dreamed of? Something inside me stirred. Was it because I was turning forty later that year? Was it because I could see my marriage coming to an end? Standing in the thick of it, like standing near the edge of the ocean where the waves crash and the water flies toward you before it recedes, I couldn't see it clearly. It wouldn't be long before I did.

No one would take a lesson with me, though. Kim worried it would knock out her back and then worried who would take care of her kids. And even George, Lisa's daring army-doctor husband, wasn't game.

They were happy to help me make it happen, though, and after a phone call to the surf shop, the lesson was scheduled. The next day off we went. The three of us girls walked from our spot on the beach on a Sunday morning to the Summer Sessions surf shop, leaving behind the husbands and six kids who were frolicking in the ocean.

I had no expectations. I was a little nervous but I had nothing to lose. I knew if I got up on the board I would be happy. My wetsuit zipped up, my teacher Zach handed me a board and told me to carry it. "It's yours," he said, pointing the way to the ocean across the street.

There was no crowd hovering around to watch me take my lesson, only the people I'd called family for so long. And they were there to support me in my endeavor, living vicariously through me, especially Kim, with her bad back.

Zach was half my age, a BMX racer who surfed in the summer. He taught me the pop-up on the beach, and then we set off into the water, where I lay on the board facing the beach and he watched the waves, holding onto the board to push me when it was time to go.

Atlantic Ocean waves aren't great like they are in Southern California. (I sound like I know what I'm talking about right?) There was a lot of waiting. I felt a little dizzy, my head at the horizon watching the water meet the sky.

Zach sent me out in a wave and I tumbled off the board, not getting the balance. He followed me and told me what I did wrong and we returned back to wave watching. While we waited, we talked about my work helping the suicide bereaved and as a speaker. I told him that I had just come up with a book title the day before, *Conversations with the Water*. I wasn't really sure how I would use it at that time. Zach suggested that it could have interviews with different people to whom water means something different: a meteorologist, a person who lives on the water, a surfer, and so on. I was thinking it was going to be fiction.

Although I shouldn't be surprised, the lesson turned into something totally different from what I expected. As Lisa said, "You two were out there having a philosophical discussion about life while you were surfing."

Learning to surf wasn't hard. I got it. Zach said I clearly understood the body awareness and the mental piece that rides alongside it. I managed to ride one of my first waves, surprising myself, along with Kim and Lisa who stood on the shore and watched. It was like I was floating across the water. I jumped off the board, not sure what to do when I ran out of water. Zach high fived me, called it "Sick!," and congratulated me on becoming a surfer. "The rest is frosting," I told him. "I didn't know if I could get up at all and now we'll just see what happens the rest of the hour."

I rode several more waves and, I fell off a few times. I played the game every surfer does every day not knowing what each wave will hold. Just like the game of life.

As we waited for the perfect wave, me lying on the board, Zach holding it and treading water, we continued our discussion and I realized that twenty years ago this wasn't how I would have approached the lesson. I would have been nervous, afraid of falling off the board, scared I would lose a contact lens, and definitely worried I might get whacked in the head with the board (which actually did happen). It was worth the twenty-year wait. As I slipped out of the wet suit, I wondered where I could surf next. Maybe I would buy a wet suit. Better yet, I need a beach house, I thought, and then I could buy a board and keep it there. The possibilities were endless.

There's a reason that dreams don't die. Sometimes they come back even more meaningful than when we first dreamed them.

I was so proud of myself. I had really done it. I had ridden on a surfboard. I had surfed. As I sat in a beach chair, eating an oversized slice of pizza, I was so happy. I'm sure I glowed for days from that experience.

I didn't know it then, but things had begun to change for me in ways I didn't expect. I also had no idea that more surfing was ahead. I'd been happy to do it once, and Zach suggested I could rent a board and go out on my own next time. When would be the next time? That I didn't know, and I filed it in the back of my brain.

Just a few weeks after returning to New Mexico, my marriage would be over and I'd be packing to move back to Naperville. Surfing was the furthest thing from my mind for a while.

Part II

1

My first memories of water are about photos. When I was eighteen months old, my dad took the five of us (my sister Denise wouldn't be born for three more years) to Indian Rocks Beach, Florida, near where he was working in Clearwater. He had been traveling to Florida during the week and flying home for the weekends. We went to Disney World on this trip, not long after it opened, and for years my brother lamented being deprived of a visit to Space Mountain because it wasn't finished yet.

I remember nothing of this trip, but thanks to the photos and the stories Mom tells, I know my love for water began there. Most of the photos of that trip are of me, probably the only time that happened. If I wasn't playing in the kiddie pool with my pink plastic bucket (later stolen at Centennial Beach in Naperville when I was about five, a place that would become important as I came of age), I was sitting on the floor of the motel room in my pajamas with my bucket and shovel, ready to go outside, my sun hat on my head. There are photos from the summer we moved to Naperville of me in my blue plastic wading pool on our newly built deck. Mom didn't fill it high, but it was emptied and refilled daily. I am surrounded by bathtub toys and other playthings, sitting there happily amusing myself.

A photo taken two summers later shows me in the same bathing suit surrounded by the same toys but with Denise climbing into the pool. The look on my face makes it crystal clear that I'm not happy about having to share my little pool with anyone.

I don't profess to have been the nicest sister in the world. When Denise was a baby in her walker, I would push her to the living room in the front of the house, which had no furniture at the time, so it was clear sailing to the far corner of the room. Then I would leave her there and return to the family room or kitchen. Of course she followed me and I would start it over again.

Most of my annoyance stemmed from having to share a room with Denise. As she grew older and up until her death, she was not the neatest person in the world. She had several loads of laundry on her floor the day she died. I know that's an indication she didn't plan to die that day but it's also the reality that she wasn't much into keeping things put away as I was. The older I got, the more organized I became. I was more likely to be called "Martha Junior" than "Surfer Girl." Because of Denise's messiness, I once put tape down on the big green rug in our room. I thought I was being kind by making her a path that led in and out of the room.

As the years went by though, that pool, or another version of it, became known as Long Lake Beach. It was a name I concocted. During the summer we would fill it to the second line (sometimes the third if Mom was in a good mood) and our Barbies, their families, and our plethora of Sesame Street and other character finger puppets would go "swimming" in that pool. We spent hours out there in the summer, usually rescuing certain finger puppets like Sherlock Holmes who always sank to the bottom of the pool.

Although I spent hours playing in Long Lake Beach, I didn't put my head under water until I was six. Denise was just a few months old when we took a trip to see the state capital and Abraham Lincoln's home, our first vacation as a family of six. There is home video of my older sister Karen walking me around the outside of a kiddie pool at a Howard Johnson motel in Springfield, Illinois, holding my hand and looking miserable because I constantly wanted to go to the pool and she was constantly told to take me. I loved the kiddie pool although there isn't much to do when you can't put your head under water. I still remember the lure of the "big pool," the one I wasn't allowed into at the motel. While there was no built-in pool in our yard at home Mom gave us as many opportunities as she could to experience water. When I was six and Denise was just three, Mom signed us up for swimming lessons at what was then Illinois Benedictine University (now simply Benedictine University). Because the shallow end was much deeper than we were tall, we stood on tables. I was placed in an older class until it was revealed that I couldn't put my head under water. I was transferred from the arms of one male swimming teacher to another to my sister's group. I can still smell funky lotion those teachers wore.

The big deal in that pool was going off the high dive in the deep end of which I never did. After that class, Mom moved us to the high school we would attend for continuing lessons. There I learned to tread water and perfect my skills with a kickboard.

The best part about being able to swim was the Holiday Inn swimming pool. Those were the days of the original Holidomes, the covered indoor play areas at some Holiday Inns. Holiday Inn brought the theme back in 2005, hoping to gain more booked rooms by adding water slides and re-creating the indoor play area that meant it didn't matter what the weather was like outside.

Dad booked us into Holiday Inns on most of our summer vacations. There were some annoying conditions: Denise and I had to share the very back of the station wagon, something we did well in the beginning but didn't quite manage throughout the entire trip. One of the four of us kids had to hide in the bathroom when they brought a rollaway bed because Dad told them he had three kids, not four. I usually got pushed to sleep on the floor because Karen complained I kicked too much during the night.

That's not what I remember most about our vacations, though. It's the Holiday Inn. We would look through the paper directory before the trip (after we learned to read) to see what kind of motel it was. They all had pools but was it an indoor pool? Was it a Holidome? If it was a Holidome it meant we could play miniature golf, too. As we drove closer to the motel, Dad would tell us to be on the lookout for the billboard with the large sign looming. Then we vied to be the first to spot the oversized neon sign.

Finally, once we had found our way to our room, we had to see the pool. Often we didn't stay more than one night because Dad kept us on a tight itinerary of places to stay and things to see (one trip was planned around Civil War battlefields) but sometimes he gave us (and Mom) the luxury of spending two nights in one place so we could play in the pool. My happiest family memories are shaped around these trips and the pools, mostly across the eastern half of the United States. Karen, Denise, and I swam as long as was allowed and if the weather was too cold or rainy, we stood with our noses pressed against the bars of the fence, sad that we didn't get to experience that particular pool.

Niagara Falls also was a pool haven. We didn't stay at the Holiday Inn there, probably because it was too expensive for Dad. Instead, we drove along Lundy Lane on the Canadian side of the falls, not to admire the flowers but to pick one of the motels that lined it. Of course, we always picked one that had a pool.

2

There are benefits to being an older sister, but in my case they were limited because I was actually the middle sister. My older sister Karen liked to taunt me using Denise as her accomplice. Using a tape recorder and cassette tapes of drug company medical lectures from our grandfather (how easy it was to tape over them when you placed a piece of tape on that little indentation), we would sit and pretend we were on the radio with *The Little Kid Show.* One time, the question was, "What is Karen's shoe size?" No matter what I said, I couldn't get it right. Only Denise could get the answer right. Karen didn't know it at the time but she was making me the stronger sibling because I learned to cope with losing even when I was right. She simply wanted to torture me.

Because Karen was six years older than me and ten years older than Denise, as we grew older, both she and Brian stopped taking family vacations. On one trip without them, we spent our last night after tooling around eastern Canada in Goshen, Indiana, at a Holiday Inn that had both an indoor and outdoor pool. It was unseasonably cool for August, and we chose the indoor pool.

It was there that I made Denise swim alongside me and call an Olympic swimming race, one where I would win the gold medal. I recall Denise doing this unhappily because I didn't think she was calling out enough commentary (probably because she was trying to stay afloat at the same time).

Still, she went along with it, and we did the same thing another day back at home in the plastic wading pool. I was bouncing a volleyball around while standing in the pool and had her interviewing me as a famous Olympic track star, even though not much more than my feet and ankles were in the water, nor is volleyball usually played in the water.

I didn't want to go on that trip we took to Eastern Canada, and Dad threatened to send me to summer camp instead. I slept through something called the Flowerpot Rocks in Nova Scotia but relished in being in the same country as my favorite pop star Bryan Adams.

Dad's job had recently been eliminated, and he retired from the company he'd worked for as a project engineer for thirty-some years. Money was tight, so we didn't stay in the usual Holiday Inns. Instead, Dad booked us into Red Roof Inns, which I detested because the toilets didn't have covers on them and I was constantly dropping things into the toilet when I was getting in and out of the shower. At one of these motels there was no hot water. Nothing good seemed to happen at a Red Roof Inn.

On the way to Canada, we stopped in Bangor, Maine, for the night. Surprisingly, Dad selected a Holiday Inn for that one night, and we got to go swimming. The problem was, despite it being August, we were freezing. Denise and I stood in the middle of the large pool and looked at each other. It was impossible to enjoy and we were shivering. Mom kept reminding us that Dad booked the Holiday Inn so we could swim since the Red Roof Inns didn't have pools.

We finally gave in and went inside to our room where we had MTV. This was 1986, and the music video channel was still growing. For us it was especially exciting because cable hadn't come to Naperville yet. All we had was a local station (Channel 66) that ran videos almost twenty-four hours a day, mostly ZZ Top's "Legs," so having MTV might have been the most exciting thing about that trip. It was more exciting than the boys I met in Chatham, Ontario, who were certainly not worth writing about.

*****

By the time I was finishing junior high, my only swimming adventures with my sister took place on family vacations once a year. We stopped taking them regularly when I was in high school, life having become too scattered and having changed in ways we didn't expect. Mom took a job as a reservations agent with the old Midway Airlines and flew us to multiple places, although we usually only stayed for the day and returned home in the evening.

But I had "the beach" with my junior high and later high school friends. I lived in one of the new neighborhoods in Naperville that at the time didn't have a community swimming pool. There was always talk of building one and I was envious of my friends who lived in areas that did because they could walk to their pool. It wasn't until I was an adult that I began to appreciate what I had instead. Centennial Beach was just over a mile from the house where I grew up. In the 1930s, as a gift to the city for its centennial, a quarry had been converted to an enormous swimming pool. The shallow end is on a slope making it easy for kids to access and a way to get one's feet wet on the way to the back, where we had our spot. The deep end is a fifteen-foot drop-off, where I learned to dive, thanks to a lifeguard named Mark.

The water is spring fed and the chemicals are carefully monitored. There are many things I could say about the beach but it would sound like a paid advertisement for the Naperville Park District.

I biked there every day for several summers. The park opened at 1:00 p.m. and I would leave home just as *Days of Our Lives* was ending. A group of us had begun to congregate near the deep end on the back side of the pool. We called ourselves The Beach Club and often spent time together outside of the beach as well. The beach was where we hung out, grew up, and learned about life. Several of us developed crushes on the college-age lifeguards, writing letters to them while they were in college during the school year. One friendship I had lasted until after my sister's death. In the later years, summer jobs kept us from swimming our afternoons away. Several of the boys took up beach volleyball, and what was left of the group congregated in a different area than the place we had spent all those hours. Still, when I reflect back, I see how lucky we were to have the beach and each other during those years.

3

Sometime in junior high, around the time the beach club formed, I developed my surfing obsession. If I lived on an ocean it might be easier to explain. And in the 1980s, no one was surfing on Lake Michigan. Recently, though, I saw a billboard that said "Surf Sheybogan" (Wisconsin) and when I mentioned this at a conference where I speaking, someone whooped it up in the crowd (no surprise—he was from Sheybogan).

I loved my Catch It T-shirt that I bought during that time. It was turquoise with a cartoon man on the front sitting at a diner counter eating something with his surfboard leaning up against the counter. It said, "Can't eat without it." The back was the same guy with his surfboard in bed next to him; it read, "Can't sleep without it." I had an Espirit skirt with couples dancing on it and often wore the T-shirt and a loose Forenza belt with the skirt, along with a pair of white-and-black Esprit slides. This was my signature outfit and the final piece was a pair of white oversized palm tree earrings.

I don't know just when, but I let surfing go, although I kept the Surf Naked bumper sticker my friend Karen bought for me, much to her father's displeasure. He thought it was inappropriate. Several years ago, I turned the skirt and T-shirt into two pillows; it was like giving my old clothes new life. Until my German shepherd puppy, Daisy, ate them.

*****

The summer after eighth grade was the summer I learned to dive into a swimming pool. I seem to have been a late bloomer most of my life– not tying my shoes until the end of kindergarten, not putting my head under water until the same time, not getting my driver's license until I was twenty-two. Of course some people never do those things—but those people didn't surround me. Naperville was a place where everyone was constantly trying to outdo each other, right down to the perfect manicured lawns.

It started at the beach one day. Two of my friends thought they would teach me to dive. They weren't too successful. They were trying to bend part of me over, but my body wasn't cooperating. The spot where we met daily was on the deep end side of the lifeguard chair. One of the lifeguards, Mark, came by at the end of his shift, and they asked him for help. He proceeded to spend some time with me, having me first crouch down and basically push myself into the water, then slowly work up to diving from a standing position.

Diving into fifteen feet of water is easy. When we were younger, my sister Denise once hit her head on the bottom of an indoor Holiday Inn swimming pool, leaving me terrified of diving into a shallow pool. But my friend Karin had a pool in her backyard, one with a diving board, and it was her grandfather who taught me how to dive off it. Skimming my hand across the bottom of the pool wasn't cool, though, so I stuck to diving at the beach, into the deep end. Even later when I had a six-foot-deep pool my backyard, I cringed when anyone dove into it.

You can't see anything in the deep end of the beach. Fifteen feet is a long way down, and it gets pretty dark. Fifteen feet is almost three of me; Michelle to the third. It's diving into the unknown sans the sharks and fish. When I look at my life, there are many times I've chosen to dive into that unknown, though usually strategically rather than stupidly.

Somewhere in seventh grade I began to form lofty goals and daydreams about my life. I knew then I would have to venture into unknown territory if I was to be who I wanted to be and accomplish those goals. I didn't always attain my goals, particularly in regard to my running, but that's another story. As I've gotten older however, I see that I've gotten good at plunging in and moving ahead. I often don't like it; I would rather take a breath and take a break. Yet I know that if I want to move forward, I will have to make that phone call, speak in front of that group, and do any number of things that involve a certain level of tension. Some things become easier, though, because I took that first dive. Recently I spoke in front of 1,500 people at a conference dinner. I'm diving into deep waters off higher platforms because of that first dive. Although I say it probably scares me more to dive into a shallower pool, I believe that it's also because I need to stay out of my comfort zone that I like to dive deep. There are too many things I want to do, especially because for almost twenty years I've been doing a list of things I didn't anticipate.

*****

In January of my freshman year of high school, Mom took the job with Midway Airlines, then the major airline at Midway Airport, on the south side of Chicago. She worked on the phone as a reservations agent and besides an income, she wanted to take advantage of the travel opportunities that working for an airline would provide. Air travel in the late 1980s was much different than today. It was more enjoyable; we didn't take off our shoes at security and we didn't have laptops to remove from our bags. Families strolled through security to get that last goodbye in at the gate or to greet loved ones returning . Mostly, planes weren't quite so full.

We took many trips in those few years Mom worked for Midway, adjusting to dressing up to board the plane and worrying we might not make a flight because we were flying standby. One summer she took Denise and me to Florida. We drove south from the airport in Jacksonville and spent one night in St. Augustine before plopping ourselves in Daytona Beach, on the shore for several days.

In the hotel pool, Denise and I met several boys. They lived in Daytona Beach and frequented the hotel pool because they could. Not our crowd. Still my best memories were of us playing in the waves. Never having had that backyard pool and only allowed to fill up Long Lake Beach to the third level, we were finally at the ocean, the best possible playground.

In 2002 I bought plane tickets to Vero Beach, Florida, to visit friends and to celebrate the end of my then-husband's cancer scare. He'd had a large growth removed from his back, and the dermatologist hadn't realized how deep it went. She was convinced it was cancer, and we waited for two weeks to find out it was benign. To celebrate, I decided we were going to the beach.

While Joe sat on a towel on the shore, I played in the waves, giggling and laughing like a ten year old even though I was really thirty. I felt as if I had slipped out of reality, or the present time, when I thought I heard Denise laughing with me. It was as if we were playing in the waves together, one of several times when her presence came through strong and clear.

I took several shells home to New Mexico and on my next trip to Chicago placed them on her headstone. She couldn't go to the beach with me the way she used to, but I could still bring some of the beach to her in a symbolic way.

Part III

1

I never thought suicide would touch my life. It's not that I thought my life was perfect. I just thought something like suicide happened to the family down the street or on the Tuesday Night Movie. But when it happened to me, it completely altered my world.

At least that's what I thought for a long time. The further I got from it, the more speaking I did, the more I experienced, the more I saw that it didn't define me. It wasn't who I truly was. But it was a journey to get to that place.

*****

After my first book, *Do They Have Bad Days in Heaven? Surviving the Suicide Loss of a Sibling* was published, everyone said I should be on Oprah. Somehow I never made it. I had people writing letters to Oprah, sending her e-mails, believing my story needed to be told. Nothing. I wrote essays, query letters, and contacted various outlets to get my story told. The big stuff never happened.

A stigma still exists around suicide and it wasn't until I had already begun to transition out of the work in the field that I began to see that it will never be completely overcome. Instead, I realized that the best way I could help the field was by doing the other work that I felt compelled to do, the work that takes me beyond suicide and circles around hope and living an authentic life. Whether I want it to or not, parts of my work will always incorporate the loss of my sister. It will be "the story" of how I have come to do what I do, even though I know that is an oversimplification. I also understand that my work in the field helped me hone my skills speaking and writing to a niche audience. The work I have done has prepared me for something bigger.

As I reach a bigger audience, one that will still learn about my sister, more people will hear more about the story and thus hear about Denise. Suicide is something that affects everyone in some way– whether we lose someone to suicide, know someone who has attempted suicide, have suicidal thoughts, attempt suicide, or try to help someone who has subsequently died by suicide. We all should know how to do what the suicide prevention training organization Living Works calls Suicide CPR. We all should know the warning signs of suicide and how to ask someone if he or she is suicidal.

When I was in Australia recently, I spent twenty minutes on the phone with a producer of a morning television show, spinning suicide several different ways. The next day he came back and said they didn't feel it was "appropriate for the breakfast crowd." That was the most appropriate time! After all, it's a time when it would reach more families and more people.

How different the lives of many people would be if someone took the chance and talked about it.

2

But after writing and speaking about suicide for almost twenty years, I don't want to do it anymore. For years, I was happy to write and speak about it because it was a way for me to explore it, learn from it, and share what I had learned. I found so much hope in the experience of grief. We often hear the sad times are what make us able to appreciate the happy times. For me it's more than that. No matter how bad I feel, there is always a glimmer of hope in those situations.

I can still remember my last high school track meet. I was devastated that I hadn't made the state track meet, that my high school running career, something that had meant so much to me, was over. I was crying on the bus on the way back to our town when something inside me changed. I was sad and I allowed myself that, but I also thought of all the other things ahead for me. Graduation was a few weeks away. My life was actually beginning, not ending. I was writing a novel, and now I would have time for that. In my grief and sadness, the sun was peeking through and reminding me that it was still there, filled with hope.

In my most recent talk, one of the last I would do specifically about grief, at the Compassionate Friends Conference banquet in summer 2012, I began to talk about surfing. While I didn't mind only discussing grief, which up to then had always been my theme, now I found myself wanting to share so much more. Amazingly, about half the people who came to speak with me after the banquet wanted to talk surfing.

Sitting in a Mexican restaurant in Santa Fe, New Mexico, Diana Sands, an Australian colleague of mine who was on vacation with her husband, suggested that I should do a new edition of my first book, *Do They Have Bad Days in Heaven? Surviving the Suicide Loss of a Sibling*. "You should write a chapter about where you are now."

I adamantly said no, I had no intention of doing anything with the book, especially because now that I've traveled almost twenty years since Denise's suicide, I don't peek inside that book, knowing that I would write something very different today.

But I know that I have been lucky. A friend who is a therapist once said how honored she is to walk the journeys she does with people who are struggling and come to her for help. In many ways I have had the same honor because people share their most painful moments with me. They give me the opportunity to learn from them. And that has allowed me to see how my words can inspire others.

The only one time in my life I considered becoming a psychologist was in fifth grade for Halloween. I'm not sure what I thought it meant other than wearing a nice dress and carrying a notepad and pen. I never wanted to sit with people in their pain although many people did it for me, but at some point I knew it was important I give back what others gave to me.

I have been all over the world and heard stories of the pain of losing a loved one to suicide and the struggle to keep hopeful in the midst of that pain. I have sat with a woman in Australia on a beach on the South Pacific eating lunch and discussing our journeys. And I have driven on the dirt roads of the Navajo Nation in New Mexico and listened to stories of suicides, stories Navajos culturally aren't supposed to speak of because their belief is that speaking about such a death will keep that person from moving on in the afterlife. But people tell the stories because they need relief, and I was lucky they shared their stories with me.

3

The summer after my junior year of high school, Mom took Denise and me to Denver. We drove south to Colorado Springs where we took the tour of the U.S. Olympic Training Center. I was hooked; I wanted to live there. I stood on the middle of the track and looked at Pike's Peak, the top covered with snow. I wanted to spend time there one day.

And the summer after Denise died, I did. My application to do my journalism internship at the OTC was accepted, and I was bound for Colorado Springs. It wasn't an easy summer, I felt alone being away from my friends in a time where e-mail was still mostly nonexistent and none of us had cell phones, and I stole as much time as I could at the AT&T five-minute phone in the lobby of the registration area. Any of us could make calls there but we were limited to five minutes because it was for anyone staying or living at the OTC. I would sneak over there on my breaks from my job as a communications intern at USA Boxing and stay on the phone as long as possible because there was usually no one in line behind me.

While it was a difficult summer, I relished spending time among the athletes, although by then the track that I loved and looked forward to running on had been replaced by an indoor swimming pool facility. Despite my sadness, I found hope in the mountain views, the dry summer air, and being surrounded by motivated and inspiring groups of people. Although some people might have said I would have fared better spending the summer at home working at the Park District on the Riverwalk, trimming shrubs as I had done the year before, I knew that I was where I was supposed to be. Letters poured in from my friends—after all, who didn't want mail that included "U.S. Olympic Training Center" in the return address?

I didn't know it at the time, but this would be the opening to other Olympic experiences. While I dreamed of competing in the games as a runner, in 1996 I was asked to work on the boxing press information team, a paid position at the Atlanta summer games. For three weeks I lived boxing, tiring of the boxed meals we were given, but again relishing the experience I felt fortunate to be a part of.

I didn't think that could be topped, but one morning in 2002 I received a FedEx package informing me that I'd been selected to carry the Olympic torch in the 2002 Salt Lake City Winter Olympics torch relay. My older sister's then-partner Jenni had nominated me, citing my work with the suicide bereaved and connecting my Olympic experience with Denise.

Denise and I had grown up watching the games. She was the sister I made swim alongside me calling the swimming race where I would win the gold medal. Twice she went with me to the Olympic Training Center. She was with me at the OTC that summer, in Atlanta, and she would be with me for the torch relay. I carried a photo of her in my sock, symbolizing her running with me. A brick inscribed with her name sits in Centennial Park in Atlanta.

Each experience I had as my life drew forward after her death made me see that she was still part of it. The day I received the call that I had been selected for the journalism internship at USA Boxing, I jumped across the couches of my apartment on the third floor repeatedly. Denise had died just three weeks before and it was the first time that I knew she was still with me. She knew how badly I wanted to spend time at the OTC. In the midst of my sadness, embers of hope still glowed.

4

Teaching high school Health and English, coaching track and cross-country, public speaking, writing nonfiction, running a state suicide prevention coalition, becoming president of a nonprofit organization devoted to suicide prevention—none of these were on my list of things to do. The list mostly consisted of things like, "Write best-selling books, write screenplays turned into Oscar-winning movies." Since first grade I had wanted to tell stories through writing. I wanted to move people, make them laugh or cry, or both. I didn't anticipate I would do it through telling the story of the death of my sister, though.

When she died, my only goal was to understand why. Reading my daily journal, the one I'd kept since junior high, showed repeated questions, trying to comprehend why Denise, my sister who I thought valued life more than anyone I knew, would die by suicide. I was lucky that a high school friend, one who was studying psychology, told me not to think about helping others until I had taken care of my own grief. Helping other people wasn't on my radar. This was the single most important piece of advice anyone gave me on the grief journey and one that served me well. It wasn't until several years later that I concocted the idea of writing a book for sibling survivors of suicide. And it wasn't until after the book came out that everything else began to fall into place.

It started with several national speaking engagements although my big book signing, to be held at the Nichols Library in my hometown, was unfatefully (yes, that's my word) held on September 11, 2001. Several other signings in my hometown were thwarted by weather and later, after finally getting past my irritation, I joked that my talks were ruined by terrorism or weather.

Things began to happen in New Mexico, though, and I found myself on the ground floor of making it happen. I was running around to meetings, and it felt like things were moving forward. And for a time we were. There was a lot of interest in the topic, and a documentary about youth suicide in the state helped. We formed a nonprofit, the New Mexico Suicide Prevention Coalition, and a second one for the suicide bereaved, New Mexico Suicide Survivors.

I lobbied legislative committee meetings, holding up a national Faces of Suicide Quilt devoted to siblings who had died by suicide. Later we had our own New Mexico quilt, with a yellow and red border, the colors of the state flag. And when a bill funding suicide prevention more generously than in any other state passed in 2004, I found myself the recipient of some of the funds.

My colleague JoAnn and I, thrown together because another colleague had written an abstract for a social work conference where we were to present together, found ourselves traveling the state. Her work focused on suicide prevention while mine was postvention (the aftercare following a suicide). She worked with kids, I worked with adults. We were the perfect team, and we enjoyed our time together, using hours of driving through New Mexico's open space to talk about our husbands, our dogs, our dreams, my pool, her house in Florida. We've been lost together on Indian reservations and pueblos and she knew when to gently pull me away from someone who wanted to share his or her story, reminding me that we needed to hit the road toward our next stop. She remains one of the few people I will share a hotel room with.

We had several contracts with the state and one with the Indian Health Service. I got to know New Mexico in a way that I never knew my home state of Illinois. We were invited into all the pueblos in the state to do what we called "Suicide 101" presentations: three hours of everything we could cover about suicide. Later we would travel to the Navajo Nation several times to do similar workshops. We knew we were fortunate to be invited to speak on sacred ground, especially as outsiders. In a meeting several years before the one that led to the IHS contract, I had been asked if I was a "Fed." As the lone white person in the room (I prefer the term "cracker," which one my students taught me when I was teaching high school), one of the Native Americans looked at me when I walked in and asked, "Are you a Fed? You look like a Fed." At the time, I had no idea what that term meant, but through the years I came to understand it was simply that I was a cracker.

No one ever treated me badly and people were very welcoming. One of my favorite experiences was one of our last. We traveled to Reserve, New Mexico, a small mountain town that had had several youth suicides. A group of people, mostly women, wanted to have a community event around the issue and had secured the funding through the county. When we showed up, they were arriving in their pickup trucks and pulling out large aluminum containers filled with enchiladas and desserts. They had created a dinner around the event, not just feeding the community's need for information but also feeding its soul.

The last workshop we did together took place in Alamo, New Mexico, a small piece of the Navajo Nation that is separated from the rest of the reservation. It is the one place in the state where my cell phone didn't work. We were scheduled for two workshops there, one during the day and one in the evening. The one during the day went fine but when it came for the evening one, no one showed. We had done workshops before where just a few people showed up but this was the first to which no one came.

Sitting outside recreation center, a beautiful facility that was clearly underused, we felt the apathy in this small community. It was a far cry from what we had experienced in Reserve but the reality for so many places.

While it takes a village for anything to happen, some of the villagers have to show up to make anything happen. I saw a little bit of everything in those years of teaching people about suicide.

5

I had no logical reason to sign the pool contract on Christmas Eve 2002. While we had been talking about putting a pool in and had bids from several company, we didn't have the money. But with Joe's head injury earlier that year—the result of being hit by a drunk driver—I was struggling with the need to balance living in the present with a future that always felt uncertain. Life, it seemed, kept trying to knock me down. I often felt like a Weeble and joked that I would "wobble but not fall down."

After the pool had been paid for, constructed, filled, and the chemicals balanced, I could see it out my office window. No one had a greater view than I did each day.

I was sitting in my office late one afternoon, the door shut so the dogs Chaco and Nestle wouldn't disturb the radio interview I was doing. We were discussing my sister's death and the associated suicide grief. The pool had just finished filling that day and I looked out the window to see the light on in the pool. Although it wasn't dark yet, all I could think was how significant this pool was to my relationship with my sister.

It had been our dream to have a backyard pool although we were always told that wouldn't happen. After she died, it was still my dream to have that pool, and here I was with a pool in my backyard. It was just as important as the day the copies of my first book, *Do They Have Bad Days in Heaven? Surviving the Suicide Loss of a Sibling* had arrived on the UPS truck. While I knew it was possible, something inside me kept thinking and believing deep down, that I didn't deserve it. I didn't think it would really happen.

But it did. I had published a book and I had the pool. I began to truly believe anything was possible in my life.

As I sat there on the phone though, I didn't know how the light went on in the pool. I wondered if the electrical guy had put it on a timer as I remembered the sales guy had said it would be set to a timer. At least that's what I swore he said.

When the interview was over, I opened the door to my office and flew down the hall to Joe who was cooking dinner. "The pool light is on!" I exclaimed, jumping around the kitchen.

Wiping his hands on a dish towel he calmly said, "Yeah, because I turned it on."

It wasn't on a timer. Why do I always think I'm right? Of course my memory fails me sometimes.

But it didn't matter. I finally had my pool.

6

There are people who realize soon after the death of a loved one by suicide that they want to help others. They don't think about their grief because they only want to make sure no family goes through what they have been through. They want to tell everyone about suicide and how devastating it is: schools, therapists, community groups, newspapers, legislators, anyone who will listen and who could make a difference.

That wasn't my experience at all. In my journal from the year after Denise died, I repeatedly asked the question, Why? Why did she end her life? Why why why? I wondered what my life was worth if she ended hers.

I was fortunate to remember the advice of my high school classmate who told me early in my grief that if I wanted to help others, I must make sure to work through my grief first. "You're no help to others if you haven't coped with your own grief," she said.

Those words resonated with me and I have passed them on to many people over the years. In some way my journalism dream died in the months after Denise died, but I knew I had to finish the degree because I had one year left. My writing didn't have the same meaning after Denise died. I decided to become a high school teacher and a cross-country and track coach. I went on to earn a master's in health education and found myself in a high school classroom in Albuquerque, New Mexico, where I had landed for graduate school.

It wasn't a disaster. I won't ever say that. It was difficult, though. I had been raised in a family that valued and expected education. When my cousin asked me if I was going to college, I looked at her and wondered, *If?* The expectation was that we went to college and got a degree. The only question was, Which college?

My Albuquerque students came from poor families, many of whom had emigrated from Mexico. One girl wanted badly to go to college but her father worked in the cafeteria at one of the hospitals and he didn't understand it. Another student showed me the rugs she wove when she spent weekends with her family on the Navajo Reservation. Their backgrounds were different from mine. Often, I was the only blonde in the room.

I had this idea that Denise's story would radiate off me when I used it to talk about suicide during the death and dying unit that I taught as part of health class. I had great teachers and coaches in the schools Denise and I attended. I am who I am because of the encouragement and belief they gave me. At the time I thought maybe Denise missed something there. I realized later it had nothing to do with the school or the teachers. As one teacher said, "We weren't worried about her work. We knew she could do that. We were worried about her."

It was a path I had to travel, though, and it brought me to an important insight. I realized that the one day I talked about Denise—what happened to her and how it tore my sports journalism career from me—was the only day I could keep the students quiet. I have the voice of a coach, I can yell like you wouldn't believe. On that day I didn't have to yell. I had something else.

I was starting to realize that I wanted to unite other sibling survivors of suicide. I knew that my siblings and I weren't the only ones who had suffered that type of loss. Yet in those days before the Internet (as impossible as that seems now), we had no way to connect. I attended a support group in Colorado Springs and then one in Albuquerque, yet not until almost two years later did I meet another sibling survivor of suicide.

At that time, my only goal was to write a book for sibling survivors of suicide. If I could accomplish that, I didn't see there was much else I could do. It took five years from the time I finished my master's degree in health education, from the day I sat in the classroom with Ron Warren, under whom I was student teaching, and told him I knew I was going to write the book.

Teaching was difficult for me because my students' lives were so different from my upper middle class background. I soon learned that my story couldn't radiate off me to students who weren't going to college and hadn't learned to write a five-paragraph essay. But because my talk about suicide, the warning signs and what to do, and about Denise's story were able to keep my students quiet, I knew I had something to work from. I don't believe anything in life happens in vain, and it turned out that for me, teaching was a path toward my book.

After I quit teaching to help my new husband start up his sales business, I offered to speak for free to other high school health classes. I'd tried to find a publisher for the book but was having little luck. The audience wasn't big enough, the letters came back saying. My book proposal showed that wasn't true–but I just couldn't make it happen.

In the summer of 1999, I joined the American Association of Suicidology. When the letter came from then-president Karen Dunne-Maxim, a fellow sibling survivor of suicide, asking how she could help me in any way, I took the offer and ran with it, sending her a few chapters of the book and forgetting about it.

In December as I was scrubbing the kitchen floor for Joe's long-awaited college graduation, I thought about how much of our lives revolved around him. I was helping build his business; I helped him finish college. It took him sixteen years and he only finished because I wrote the last paper. I often joked that his degree should have had my name on it, too. But as I was washing the floor, thinking about the party we were having that night and about how much of our life together was about him, that's when Karen called me and invited me to speak, although for only about seven minutes, at the American Association of Suicidology conference the next year in Los Angeles.

My favorite place in the world, Los Angeles, and an opportunity to share my work. Finally. It was there that I met Jack Bolton, whose wife, Iris Bolton, is well known in the world of suicidology. In the early 1980s, the Boltons had attempted to find a publisher for Iris's book about the suicide of their son, Mitch. With no luck, they started Bolton Press Atlanta, and it was Jack who approached me about publishing my book.

Finally, when people called telling me they needed my book, I would be able to promise that a book was on the way rather than shaking my head and explaining how I couldn't find a publisher.

In July 2001, the UPS truck delivered several boxes of my book to the house and I sat on the back porch looking through it.

"What do you think? Are you happy?" Joe asked.

"I'm worried the font is too big," was all I could say. He laughed, and friends brought a cake to celebrate.

While much frustration would follow the publishing of the book—it's one thing to publish a book but another to market it, and suicide is not just a niche audience but a topic filled with stigma—many opportunities were waiting for me just around the corner.

Joe had taught me that if you kept working at something the rewards would come (throwing shit against the wall was what he actually said, and that some of it would start to stick). What should have been my big book signing in Naperville at the library fell on 9/11. The 9/11. I had done WGN morning television the day before, there had been several newspaper articles, and we all thought this was my big moment. I knew I was lucky to have thirty people there but I was disappointed. When we tried it again in the spring, we had a snowstorm.

Word about the book was getting around the suicide grief community. It was a first for sibling survivors of suicide, and the speaking engagements followed.

By 2003, I found myself in the midst of work in New Mexico and I wasn't sure when the road would end.

7

Leadership is always an honor. It's a reward for a job well done, whether at a fast food restaurant or in the corporate world. I never saw myself as a leader in high school. When running took over my life, I worked hard because it was what I wanted. In the spring of my senior year, I was rewarded with a captain's pin for my varsity letter.

This was an honor but it was also difficult for me. I was a silent leader and struggled with being outwardly supportive of my teammates. It wasn't that it was hard; instead it felt unnatural. I thought long and hard and realized that it was something I wasn't able to do. I returned the pin to our head coach, Mr. Moody.

He was disappointed, I'm sure, but he probably also saw that I had made the mature decision not to do something I didn't feel was right for me.

As the years went by, I would find myself repeatedly placed in positions of leadership, but it wasn't until after Denise died that I found I was ready for them, especially the years after my book was published. Maybe by then I felt I had something to offer, although I believe it's more that I was a late bloomer in everything. Now there were things that needed to be done, opportunities to be seized, and I took them, not wanting to miss them. I became president of the New Mexico Suicide Prevention Coalition, not because I wanted to but just because I knew I could do it. And if I didn't gather the group together to found New Mexico Suicide Survivors, I didn't see how anyone else was going to make it happen.

I began to see that my role in many ways is to connect people—first on the local level but then at the state level, the national level, and later internationally. I still didn't see myself as a leader, though, so much as someone who wanted to get things done.

Good leaders are hard to come by, and in 2007, I was approached about running for President-Elect of the American Association of Suicidology. I had been talking about backing away from the work but apparently there was still something for me to do and I ran. And won.

At the same time, I had picked up international work and felt a renewed sense of meaning. By this time I felt I had done all I could locally and handed off both the state suicide prevention coalition and NMSS. A good leader knows when it's time to move on, and I felt I needed to do bigger things.

It lasted for a while but I still had a feeling that there was something else for me to do. The state legislature had appropriated a large sum of money to our organization, and some of it was coming to me to do workshops with my colleague JoAnn. But it was feeling stale to talk about suicide, especially about my sister's death, something that had happened more than fifteen years before. I wondered if Tanya Tucker ever felt that way about singing "Delta Dawn" from the time she was sixteen.

I finished my doctorate and started to dabble in talking about dog companionship. I became pickier about what speaking engagements I accepted. During this time my first book continued to sell. People friended me on Facebook for my work and told me how I inspired them.

It felt like I was cookie dough that someone was mixing. The mixture continued to churn. I was changing.

8

On New Year's Day 2006 my father died of a heart attack. It was unexpected, although we could look back and see that he was sensing his time to die was coming. He told me just two weeks before his death that if he should die, he was ready. He was struggling with his new false teeth, and his feet hurt.

In many ways it was like the day that Denise died. I had my thoughts on the list of things I was going to work on that day. There were bowl games to watch, a quilt to sew, and a fridge filled with leftover Mexican food I'd made for a dinner party the night before. All was well until my older sister called to tell me they were on their way to the hospital because Dad had collapsed.

Not that we're ever ready to lose a loved one— as my friend JoAnn says, death is never convenient—but I wasn't ready for my dad to die. I had just turned thirty-five. I wasn't ready for the Father's Day card aisle and the commercials on television to make me unhappy. There would be no father in my life to celebrate with now that he was gone.

It was different from losing Denise, but not because they were at different ends of their lives. Dad's death made me forget about her death. While sometimes death takes us back to the trauma of a previous one, this time I didn't feel that. Instead I struggled to understand how the bond between my father and me had changed. I knew it hadn't broken.

While people are often told after the death of a loved one to break the attachment to the deceased, that the person is gone and they need to let go, I have never believed that. I feel lucky to live in a time where our focus is on continuing bonds and how we do things to make that happen.

I thought of none of this after Dad died, though. All I could think about was how I was going to adjust to life without him. I didn't think of it in these words, but what I was wrestling with was how that bond had changed and how to adjust. I had too much going on in my life to stop and investigate. Nor did I want to stop. I was working on my doctorate and planned to take my comprehensive exams at the end of the semester. Suicide was a hot topic in New Mexico, and I had multiple contracts to fulfill.

Two years later, Joe and I would watch our German shepherd Daisy slowly die from hemangiosarcoma, a cancer that attacks the blood vessels. She was five and a half years old. After we took Daisy to the veterinarian's office to euthanize her, I went home feeling completely lost. I went to the grocery store. I vacuumed the floors. I hated that place you're at when the death is over, when the funeral is over, when you wonder what we do next.

I had to adjust to life without Daisy. And yet I also felt that I needed to do something with her death. I had to make sense of it. I thought about writing about her and subsequently did write several articles, focusing on what we learned from coping with a terminally ill dog.

Denise's death had become a part of my past. I no longer felt it. The pain of losing her was long gone. I knew she was there to greet Dad and she and Dad were later there to greet Daisy. When I lost two uncles in a six-month period a few years later, I began to feel as though I had more family in the afterlife than here with me on earth.

No matter who died, though, I felt a need to write about it and put it somewhere. There had to be something to learn in each of these deaths, and the only way I knew how to work with that was to keep writing.

9

The transition from a suicide and grief focus in my life didn't happen overnight. I didn't wake up one morning, realize that I had done everything I was supposed to do in the suicide and grief field, and proceed to move on. The change started slowly and evolved over a period of time, especially because suicidology kept luring me back in. I would tell people I was leaving, and then something would draw me back. Frank Campbell, best known for his work creating LOSS Teams that reach out to the suicide bereaved on the scene of a suicide, had come to Albuquerque to give a talk. He and I were sitting at the Flying Star on Central Avenue having lunch.

"Suicide has to become a smaller part of the pie that makes up my life," I told him. "It's time for me to do other things."

No one disagreed. But then it was only 2007 and there was still much more for me to do. Later that summer, I found myself in Killarney, Ireland, speaking at the International Association for Suicide Prevention conference. There I would meet several international colleagues and return home with new energy and new hope for work in the field.

But it was also during this time that I began to see my grief journey in a different light. And not until fifteen years had passed, the same fifteen years during which I began to feel the suicide piece of my life getting smaller, did I realize how much running had helped me cope with Denise's death. I didn't stop running—not even the days after her death when I felt as if the world had stopped turning on its axis and someone forgot to tell me. Feeling as if I was running crooked, I kept doing it.

In my workshops I began to focus on the importance of taking care of oneself not just emotionally, but also physically. "Get out and go for a walk, smell and feel nature around you," I would tell people. It was because no matter how bad I felt, no matter how much I didn't want to get up and run, I still did it because I knew that it forced me to be present in nature, something one can't do curled up in bed.

I read a novel about grief once where a woman loses her husband and talks about being curled up in bed with chocolate ice cream. I never finished the book nor did I write my first novel about dealing with grief that way. I don't understand how writing about someone who hides from life can teach readers about grief. I didn't want to go out running, but I knew I had to keep doing it. While Rachel, my character in *The Australian Pen Pal*, wasn't a runner or exerciser, she didn't stay in bed except to sleep. She had a garden to tend to, a life to live, and books to write. And she didn't eat gallons of chocolate ice cream to make herself feel better. Instead, she invited her friends over and fed them Mexican food and served them margaritas.

As I began to realize that my work around suicide and grief was changing, it also made me more aware of how my grief might have been different from other people's. Often people asked me how I coped. In the first years, I would say that writing in my journal, writing an ongoing letter to Denise, and talking about her death with my friends and other people were key.

On some level, I also knew running was important. I struggled that first summer after her death, running at altitude for three months in Colorado Springs. I got up early, often leaving the complex before six a.m., depending on how many miles I wanted to run that day. There were some days I walked, though, my eyes filled with tears as I fought to understand why Denise ended her life and changed mine. Later that fall, back at Ball State, I would stop on the sidewalk in front of the football stadium, crouch down, and cry. Cars passed. I kept crying. Finally I got back up to run back to my apartment.

I kept running. I love to run although some days I battled it, coping with the various injuries that happen when you turn an ankle or slip on ice. Running and I didn't always get along, but I kept doing it because it fed me like an addictive drug, although that would ease off as the years went by. I still had to run each day, but I would learn that the occasional day off was okay (especially when I flew overseas at night and arrived in another country early the next morning).

I started running the summer after sixth grade when I asked my mom to sign me up for the local park district track and field camp. She bought me a pair of primitive-looking blue Nike running shoes, and off I went.

I was never much of an athlete. I was more likely to get hit in the head by a ball than kick it or catch it. I was a terrible runner. What I did have was long stick legs and a drive that was waiting to burn inside me.

Somewhere I became a running addict. I didn't know it at the time but it taught me more about life than anything else up to that point. I didn't always like it, and I sometimes looked for something else to take its place (race walking and cycling were two options that never panned out), but it was if the bond between running and me was too strong. I couldn't let go.

When I was writing my first book, a non-athlete friend complained I used too many sports references. I described solving problems and overcoming obstacles as "getting over hurdles." This was not surprising since I had been on the road to becoming a sports writer, so I wasn't about to delete those metaphors. They were coming from me, and that was how I defined myself.

For years I struggled with what I didn't accomplish as a high school runner. I quit competing after my freshman year of college but continued to run daily. It was as much a part of me as brushing my teeth. And it wasn't until many years later, when people began to ask me what helped me cope with the death of my sister, that I realized that running was my most important tool.

One of the basics of distance running is learning not to stop. You have to fool your brain, and one of the ways you do that is by giving it objectives, goals to run to. It could be running from mailbox to mailbox or tree to tree. Or even a mailbox to a tree. You pick something in the distance, tell yourself to run to it, and when you get there, you look for something else to run to.

Dealing with grief is like that. Grief is taxing, and after a loved one dies, it's exhausting to think about waking up to the long day ahead. We have to break the day down into smaller units so it's not overwhelming. We might need to go hour-to-hour or even minute-to-minute. Whatever it is, the big goal has to become smaller goals. That way we find we can survive, just as when we are running and want to stop, looking at the mailbox that's close by is easier than thinking about our driveway three blocks away.

Running also taught me that even when I feel like I can't go on, I can. Some of the toughest cross- country and track workouts we had were repeat 400s. A 400 is one lap around the track, and we would do those maybe eight or nine times. Early in the season they were done with little rest to build up our endurance but near the end of the season they would be done with long rests because a faster pace was expected.

I would reach the middle and think, I've done four, how can I do five more? I want to die. I want to lie down on the track and never get up again.

That's how we feel sometimes in grief. We think, I can't do this anymore. I can't go on anymore. It's too painful without my loved one. There are many life situations where we feel that. Life feels too overwhelming and we're tired.

But what do we do? It's expected that we will finish the workout. It's expected that we will get up and go on. We have a million reasons why we can't give up, and we don't. In running, it might be a coach who expects us to finish, but we owe it to ourselves to complete the run. And it's the same in life; our family might expect us to keep going but really we owe that to ourselves.

And when we keep going, when we survive and see that we can get through full days without wondering how we will do it, we realize that we are much stronger than we thought we were. We might reflect back and wonder how we did it but we do know that if we survived that grief for a loved one, we can survive anything else that life hands us.

Running taught me to be present in life but also to let go of whatever I was feeling and get lost in the seasons. While the rest of me kept working emotionally coping with my loss, running kept my physical self going. And it did much more than that.

10

In the fall of 2008 I found myself spending a week in rural Ohio, north of Columbus, speaking to several high schools about suicide. It was a rare opportunity because schools are often reluctant to have anyone speak about suicide, afraid of what the outcome will be. But the woman who had arranged for me to speak had convinced eight high schools in the county that it would be good to have me talk to their students. Each school had a counselor ready for any students who needed help afterward. Yes, when someone comes to speak about suicide, students do come forward to ask for help, and that's a good thing. Convincing a school administration, however, isn't always easy.

I told a little of my sister's story but I also talked about the things that helped me cope– writing and running. One school was a state power in cross-country, and the counselor especially wanted one student to hear my message since he was also interested in journalism.

I relished the opportunity to speak to these students, and also to speak to a small college in the area where they had sadly just had a suicide the week before. I had long ago learned there are no coincidences. This had been on my calendar for a year; the suicide was only a week old.

During this time, as I was speaking to the students, I also was beginning to see what an important part running had played in my grief and in who I was. Not until 2011, though, did I begin to let go of some of the suicide/grief activities in which I was involved. I knew that I had to close some doors to open others. I might miss out on the opportunities I really wanted if I didn't close those doors.

I also realized that it was time for me to publish my fiction. I didn't want to wake up realizing that it was too late to publish, that I hadn't accomplished one of my most important goals. It was the ambition that had kept me going since I was six years old. Even on my darkest days, when my life was filled with loss, change, and transition, the desire to tell stories burned deep inside me. All these characters were alive in my brain, and I needed to tell their stories.

I put out *The Australian Pen Pal*, first as an ebook, and followed it with the paper copy when people started to ask for it. The day that I sent it to the publisher, a Sunday morning in my office where my designer Megan and I were going back and forth over the final changes, I clicked that button and sat back in my desk chair. In that moment, I realized that I had just accomplished something huge in my life.

When I walked away from my desk, I also realized it was the same week I would become president of the American Association of Suicidology. I had never dreamed of being president of AAS. It was a research organization, and I wouldn't be like the previous presidents. The field was ready for something different. I had a PhD, but I was not an academic. I was a writer and speaker, the public face of suicide loss and the hope that one can find in life.

I didn't sense it as such right away, but my work over the next two years would be the end of my road in the field. Later that summer when my marriage ended and I found myself packing up my life and moving it back to Chicago, more doors began to close, and I had to wait patiently for the new ones to open.

11

As my path was shifting, several times people said how much they loved the bright dresses I wore when I spoke to an audience. Knowing what I spoke about, they didn't expect me to look so . . . happy in my photos.

This was who I was, though. In college, when the letter I wrote to Denise just two weeks after her death was published, I had long since gone to bed when the page layout was completed at *The Daily News*. The next morning I was told of the debate about whether or not to use the photo of me for the column. Some people were against it because I looked happy in the photo and it didn't match the topic. Others disagreed, pointing out that this was how I looked and adding that it would personalize the story. The letter ran without my photo.

Smiling and wearing bright dresses is who I am, though. I had my own style in junior high, wearing The Limited's Forenza brand pencil skirts rather than jeans. However, by the time I went off to college, my style got stuck and stayed that way. Looking back, I see it also represented the time. To be taken seriously women were expected to dress like men: the corporate look. I bought into it, especially being a short blonde, and gave up my fun skirts for khaki pants. In 2007, though, my style started to re-emerge. I bought shorter shorts, lowered my necklines, and went back to my shorter skirts. Then I brightened the colors I chose to wear.

Pink had been a part of my early life thanks to my love for Barbie, but in those years after college, I thought I couldn't wear any pastel color. I gave all my pastel shirts away. Only after 2007 did I start to wake up. "The heck with it," I thought, and returned to my own style. That's when I started hearing the comments about my bright-colored dresses.

Fashion opened up to women in the corporate world, and I fell in step alongside everyone else who went for dresses rather than suits. I could wear pink in corporate America. Prints even. I felt like myself when I spoke to an audience, choosing dresses that I loved, and often garnered comments from others, men as well as women.

Although I was surprised that people told me they were surprised to see me smiling and wearing those bright colored-dresses, I also realized that it was who I am. There is nothing more important than being who we truly are.

Part IV

1

As my life went on post-Albuquerque and post my marriage, I began to understand that I had been brought back to my hometown for a reason.

I had vowed never to return to Naperville once I moved away. From seventh grade on, I'd had a dream to move to Los Angeles, although I never made it that far. My parents laughed at how I packed up everything I owned and moved it to my dorm room at North Park University, the school I attended before transferring to Ball State. I had a sense that I needed to separate myself from my life in Naperville.

After my dad died in 2006, Joe and I began to contemplate buying a second home for several reasons. I approached him about buying one near my mom, close to the house I grew up in. I found myself wanting to return there and it felt good to be back in Naperville for several weeks at a time.

In late 2010 we moved Mom into that house and I began to think that I had bought it and furnished it for her. Again, we don't often understand things we do in the midst of them. But in 2011 after the end of my marriage, it was also a place for me to go, although I knew I wouldn't stay more than a year or two.

Going forward, I felt that I had been brought back to finish things that had been cut off in the years before Denise died. The roads had converged.

I didn't anticipate how I would change when the marriage ended. I actually didn't change so much as return to the core of who I truly am. I began to see myself return to that core. At first it wasn't obvious to me, as it's usually not when we're in the thick of it.

After I moved, I took several trips for speaking engagements. First, I drove down to Ball State University, my alma mater, to speak about the road I had traveled and about suicide prevention. This was significant because that's where I was when Denise died and where I returned to speak, for about 250 students, after my first book was released. Now, almost twenty years later, the room was packed. I'd had several lackluster experiences speaking on college campuses, and I'd been told that universities weren't interested in the topic of suicide despite the increased number of programs on campuses for suicide prevention. Those speaking engagements had been disappointing, and I was surprised to see over 100 students and community members overflowing the room to hear me speak about what had happened to me while I was there as a student, how to help the suicide bereaved, and how to help someone who was suicidal. It was as if life had taken me back there one last time to speak about suicide before I moved on.

From Indiana I flew to Hawaii where a bigger change was coming although it didn't seem so large at the time.

2

My luggage didn't make it to Honolulu on the same plane with me. The wind had extended the length of the flight and I was lucky I made my connection. But arriving into a muggy Honolulu evening, all I could think about were my pajamas and my face soap. And sleep. I had done this gig a year before on my way to Nova Scotia, and when I arrived my luggage still sat in Denver. It took a full twenty-fours that time; this time I had my bag by two in the morning .

The trip to speak at a conference for the suicide bereaved had been on my calendar long before I knew I'd be moving to Chicago as a single person. And I realized that maybe I could surf on this trip. While I was there, Pua, who had asked me to come, assured me that someone in her family would take me surfing.

It was the week before Thanksgiving, and Waikiki was probably as empty as Waikiki gets. My hotel was situated at the east end of Waikiki, the quiet end, I learned. I could see the lights at night of what I called the Vegas part of Waikiki. I ran around Diamond Head each morning. Life felt lazy to say the least. "Just enjoy yourself!" Pua told me. I found I was exhausted. I'd spent the past six weeks getting ready to move and then actually moving. Finally, I had a break.

On my second afternoon, Pua called and said that her daughter would be texting me to let me know that her former son-in-law was going to take me surfing. A text from Nala said he would arrive in a red truck and to be waiting outside my hotel at 3:15. I sat on a bench wondering who was taking me surfing. His name was Sunny. I knew nothing else about him.

A red pickup truck arrived shortly, and a teen opened the passenger door and climbed into the bed. A man clad in only board shorts with an upper body covered with tattoos walked around from the driver's side and introduced himself as Sunny. We shook hands and drove to the beach.

My male friend Chris would later ask me, "You went surfing with some guy and you didn't even know his last name?" He was Pua's former son-in-law. I had no doubt that Pua would take care of me. Nala and I were the same age; Pua was like a mom to me.

Because it was mid-November, the sun was setting early on the island and I could see it dipping closer to the ocean as evening neared. There would be no need for a wet suit here, but it wasn't warm either.

Sunny said we were going to rent surfboards, and the first sign that something unusual was happening came when the boards were comped. Sunny put his money away, and then a man walked over to us with his phone and asked someone to take his photo with Sunny. Later, an older man paddleboarding stopped paddling and balanced himself on the water to shake Sunny's hand. "You're learning from the best," he said to me, pointing at Sunny.

Sunny was Sunny Garcia, the two-time world surfing champion. Later in my room at the hotel I would Google him and laugh out loud at who I had just spent an hour on the ocean with. In Los Angeles a month later I would see a billboard with Sunny surfing a wave when I was driving from San Diego to LAX to fly back to Chicago. He was the big time but to me he was simply Pua's son-in-law.

I explained to Sunny that I had only been surfing once and I lived landlocked. He worked on the popup with me again and then we paddled out into busy waters. While it was getting late in the day and I thought the water and beach were busy with people, this was nothing compared to the peak season.

Much like with Zach in New Hampshire, Sunny and I had some interesting discussions as we waited for the waves. They were tamer than usual. Pua hadn't been able to give me an exact date and time for surfing because the first event of the Triple Crown was set to start on the North Shore. Yet the waves weren't cooperating, and the event organizers were waiting for the ocean to invite everyone for the party.

Sunny learned to surf to keep out of trouble, not knowing that it would provide him with a means to make a living and support his family. He went out on a wave after me and I watched as he surfed seamlessly. I'm sure the small waves felt as easy as walking on carpet for him.

I didn't fare so well, nor did I give up. Finally, near the end of our hour and getting close to 6:00 p.m., the water was getting colder and the sun inching closer to the horizon, Sunny said to me, "Don't look down. Watch the buildings." He pointed at the hotels stretched out in front of us. I had been looking down at the water and the board.

The next time out, I surfed the wave. Finally. Everything Sunny told me was exactly what Zach had said but he'd added the piece of the puzzle about not looking down.

Later, I would hear stories that Sunny had gone to jail for fighting over waves. I never asked anyone if these stories were true although I have heard stories about lawsuits over waves in California. I never saw Sunny that way because several evenings later when I saw him at an event related to the conference, he was sitting with a baby in his lap. If he was the big bad surfer, all I saw was a kind, supportive man.

Hawaii had never been on the list of places that I dreamed of going. Those first few days in Honolulu, Pua kept telling me to relax and enjoy being there. I felt lazy but I realized that for almost two months, my life had been going nonstop. Once Joe and I had agreed to divorce, I had about a month to work at undoing everything we'd been tying together over twelve years. There were two houses, two business, four dogs. No one helped me pack up what I decided I wanted to take. I had to finish out my life in New Mexico while everyone in Chicago waited for me to arrive and become part of their lives again. A few days after my sister I and drove twenty-four straight hours, I took off for Indiana to speak at my alma mater, Ball State.

When I got home after that, my belongings had arrived, and I longed for help in organizing my possessions. I had wisely packed my bag for Hawaii before I left New Mexico knowing I probably wouldn't be able to find what I needed once I moved.

But Hawaii turned out to be just what I needed and Pua knew that, although probably not on a conscious level since the event had been planned almost a year earlier. Life was falling into place in many waves. And I'd been able to surf again.

3

In late June, I flew to Australia for the third time in five years.

Besides my work speaking at the Third Australian Postvention conference, I had several goals to accomplish while I was Down Under. The first was to make what I call my first pilgrimage in my life, to St. Mary's Cathedral in Sydney. On my previous trip several years before, I had stumbled on St. Mary's one afternoon with time to spare. The church had a gift shop where I had bought a silver rosary. As my marriage began to crumble, I found that rosary on my desk and had it blessed. At first, the plan had to been to actually pray the rosary but I realized that was unrealistic. Sometimes there are things in life that I'm just not going to do. I'd read somewhere that each bead can represent a mantra, and I used that approach to find strength as my life began to change around me. I wanted to return to the church because I sensed that it would be integral in my coping and my continuing to see hope in my life.

But before returning to Sydney from the Sunshine Coast, where I was to spend several days staying with friends, I needed to go surfing. I didn't anticipate being invited back for the fourth postvention conference since I had spoken at the first three. I had to surf before I left Australia because I wasn't sure when I would be back.

It was sunny when I arrived in Sydney on a late June winter morning. When I arrived on the Sunshine Coast north of Sydney on the South Pacific, it was like November in Chicago: dreary and somewhat wet. I felt as if I should be at home watching football on television. My friend Jill's house smelled like Thanksgiving dinner.

Jill was clear she would make surfing happen. She had once been a surfer herself and she asked her sons if they would take me out. Although their schedules didn't work, the weather for the next day didn't look as if it was going to hold and the surfing report in the newspaper indicated there wouldn't be much to surf anyway.

It ended up raining most of that day–I stayed inside and did some work and ate mandarins off the tree in the backyard. The forecast wasn't looking better for Tuesday. My Irish friend Barry was also in Australia to attend the same conference and we all laughed that it would clear up when he left. I resigned myself to the fact that on Friday I was probably going to have to surf at Bondi Beach in Sydney. I didn't want to do that because I knew it would be more crowded.

While it didn't look better on Tuesday, Jill and I agreed I would meet her at her office and I'd go to the beach and find a surf school. I planned that this would be my last lesson although I wasn't sure when I'd have another opportunity to get up on a board. I hadn't surfed since Hawaii seven months before, and I didn't feel confident yet.

Hannah, Jill's assistant, drove me to a secluded part of the beach where several vans advertising Merrick's Surf School idled. Brochures wet from the rain were smushed behind the wiper blades of parked cars.

I had no idea who Merrick was, and I didn't care. I needed to surf. My planned pilgrimage to St. Mary's would be a piece of cake after this.

Sitting in Hannah's car with a meat pie in my lap, I called Merrick. He answered the phone himself.

"I don't want a class," I told him. "I've taken lessons twice before." While it was winter and Merrick was short staffed, his daughter agreed to answer the phone so he could take me out.

I had almost two hours before the lesson and used that time for shopping. The winter rain poured down and I arrived back at the secluded site with shopping bags that were dripping wet. I knew it was Merrick in the wetsuit, smiling as I arrived looking way out of character for someone arriving for surfing lesson, I'm sure. I had my big white Benetton purse in one hand, the shopping bags in the other, and I'd changed into my bikini in the primitive bathrooms around the corner in the woods.

The rain held off for the two hours we were on the ocean, with the water warmer than the air. Despite the clouds and the roaring surf that continued to pick up as the time ticked by, I was glad I was surfing in Australia. If my trip ended the next day, even without making it to St. Mary's, I would be happy.

"My father went to buy a bucket of KFC chicken when I was kid," Merrick said, "and he got a Styrofoam surfboard with it. That's how I began surfing."

Wearing short wetsuits, we headed out to the ocean, each carrying a board. It had been frustrating not to use what I'd learned in New Hampshire and Hawaii yet I didn't feel comfortable going out on my own. How did I judge a wave? Did I even remember what to do? Merrick started from scratch and into the water we went.

"See the riptide there?" he asked pointing at a place in the water where the ocean seemed to meet like a zipper that wouldn't close. "A riptide isn't good for swimming but it's good for surfing." He pointed in the other direction, behind him, where ledge of rocks was formed. "This is a great spot for surfing." It was all because of how the waves formed in the environment that surrounded them.

Merrick's style was slightly different than that of Zach or Sunny, who mirrored each other. It didn't matter to me, though. I was a sponge and I was determined to soak up everything he taught me. It would also be nice to say I surfed in Australia. "Noosa is the place," Jill kept repeating. "You have to say you surfed Noosa."

The lesson was two hours. After the first hour, I actually thought we were done when Merrick called me to follow him out of the ocean. "Let's go get some water," he said.

Along the way he asked me what I was in Australia to speak about and then proceeded to tell me about a friend who had killed himself, leaving behind a family. There wasn't much room for me to comment, especially once we reached the water pump where another surf coach and a mother and two kids had gathered.

Back in the water, Merrick said the goal was to get me up on the board. I could feel the waves crashing harder, getting larger. "Don't be afraid!" he called from behind me, wanting me to jump into the waves with the board at my side (to avoid getting hit in the face).

I'm not scared! I wanted to call back to him. I realized it was silly that I appeared scared since jumping in the waves was what Denise and I had done all our times in the ocean together.

Merrick pushed me to go out further; he pushed me to keep going after I fell off the board each time. There was no stopping him . There were more waves to try and catch. I was forced to be lost in the moment. I knew he was cold; because the water was actually warmer than the winter air, he stayed ducked under as long as he could. I was the cold one, floating on the board waiting for the waves.

I did finally get up. Somewhat. I knew it didn't matter, though. Everyone would want to know if I got up, but Merrick was another step in my surfing journey. He taught me about safety, how to keep the board away from my face, and he pushed me to keep going.

When Hannah picked me up after the lesson, it was still pouring and I wasn't getting dry. "I think I need another meat pie," I told her, and we laughed all the way to a bakery in Noosa. Back at Jill's office, though, Jill's eyes opened wide when I told her who had taught me to surf.

"Merrick? Merrick Davis is an Australian world champion," she said. "You are obviously supposed to surf because you have all these champions teaching you."

While the driving rain almost kept me from getting back to Sydney (the gate agent didn't care that I was appearing on national television the next day, "We can't guarantee you'll make it," she kept saying), the incoming plane finally landed and it was sunny in Sydney. I attended Mass at St. Mary's and was glad I didn't have to surf at Bondi. I much preferred the peace of Noosa and the help of Merrick.

4

Twice the morning I left for Los Angeles to be the banquet speaker for the Compassionate Friends Conference in Costa Mesa, I had people ask me if I was going to surf while I was there.

And twice I told them no.

"Of course you could go surfing," Lois called from the front seat of the car where she sat in front of me, her husband Sam driving us back to their home in Palos Verdes from the airport where they'd picked me up. It was just three weeks after my trip to Australia.

After being asked about surfing the second time, I had told Lois and Sam about it. Even though I had said no, surfing had crossed my mind. As I lay in bed that morning, I thought about throwing a bikini into my luggage just in case. I wanted to blame my failure to be prepared on the fact that I had an early flight and I had forgotten, but the truth was that I didn't really think it would happen. I had writing to do before the conference, and I thought it would be a nuisance to find a board to rent and then actually get up on it.

Plus, what no one knew was that I was a little scared to go out on my own. It wasn't that I feared the ocean or being out there on the ocean by myself, it was that I still didn't quite understand how to pick the waves. I also worried about running into other surfers.

"But I didn't bring a bikini," I said.

"Then we'll stop at T.J. Maxx," Lois said.

This wasn't the big deal that I thought it was, I realized. They lived on the ocean, surfing was part of that life, and they were giving me an opportunity to have that life for a few days. I certainly wasn't going to turn them down.

Between T.J. Maxx and Target, I pieced together a bikini that made me happy for $22. A Google search later, and I had found Open Ocean Surf Shop in Redondo Beach. Within fifteen minutes, Lois and I were on our way to the shop to rent my board and wet suit.

When life gives us opportunities to step out of box, to do the things we really want to do, we shouldn't turn them down. Jamie, the owner of the store, was happy to help and Lois was a happy accomplice.

When I struggled to zip up the back of the shorty wetsuit I was trying on, I was reminded of all the times I have been alone in a hotel room, getting ready to speak, and I couldn't zip up the back of my dress; the times when I wished I had someone to help. I walked out and Jamie laughed and said, "You're going to have to learn to do this if you want to surf." He explained that was why the cord in the back is so long. Once again, I was reminded that each time I go surfing, someone is there to teach me something.

I walked out with a soft eight-foot blue board under my arm and a shorty wetsuit over Lois's arm. After purchasing a Marie Callender's cherry pie a few stores down from the surf shop, we drove back to Palos Verdes. There would be no excuses. I was going out on the water by myself.

"You don't need lessons," my friend Chris told me earlier that day, without me telling him my dilemma, knowing that I finally needed to go out on my own. "You just need to get a board and do it."

The next morning I went for a short run. I kept thinking it would be easier not to go. I knew, though, that the board and wet suit were waiting for me in the minivan. There was no turning back. I'd paid up for two days for the board and I was going to get what I'd paid for.

First I had to find the beach. Sam had drawn me a map and given me a printed map of the area. The ocean I got to fine. But walking to the beach was another story. Lois had pointed "over there" with her hand the evening before to show me where Rat Beach was. I figured it would be obvious what path to take down the hill but when I saw the sign stating "no one authorized" at the start of a paved road, it threw me. This is typical for me, as I always seem to make one wrong turn wherever I go. I had left everything but the board in the car, the key safety-pinned inside my bikini top (as a runner, I know all the tricks for keeping keys safe).

Instead of taking the road, I kept walking to where I thought there was a path through some woods. I was beginning to feel stupid that I couldn't find the beach. It couldn't be that hard. When I finally asked someone, I realized it was the paved road I was supposed to take; they just didn't want people to drive down the road.

I never reached 5' 3" and the board was not only much taller than me but also wider than my wingspan. Carrying it downhill was an adventure, and when I got to the bottom, I saw there was a long path to actually reach the beach where I would enter the water. I'm also rather competitive when I walk and I hate to be passed, even when I have a surfboard larger than me under my arm.

I hiked the board closer under my arm and, even though I was barefoot, picked up the pace. The water wasn't as crowded with surfers as I thought it might be. It wasn't like Hawaii, where Sunny had warned me that people were territorial, and later that day, Sam would tell me stories from the area that led to a lawsuit and the locals being told to back off. As a novice, I was especially worried about getting in anyone's way. Being a novice was bad enough but I'm a short blonde woman novice who can pass for someone in her twenties. There would be no way for them to know who I was, just that I was someone in their way, much like Gidget when she first showed up in Malibu and was teased by the surfers.

I needn't have worried. There was plenty of room for all of us. I stood on the beach for a few minutes watching the surfers, then practiced the popup. I pulled the wetsuit up the rest of the way over my new bikini and carried the board into the water, trying to remember all that Merrick had taught me. Hold the surfboard from the bottom to keep it upright so that it didn't whack me in the face when the waves came. Instead, it would ride the wave. Lean into the wave. I still couldn't believe I would forget to do that. But I was also thinking about the board, something I was treating like my own child since it didn't belong to me.

Toward the north, there were more surfers. Jamie advised me to surf around others but I was careful not to be too close. Mostly what I saw were surfers waiting. And waiting. And waiting. They would try a few waves but the waves would peter out. I watched for a while.

Then my struggle began. I still didn't get the wave thing. Merrick was right: during a lesson, it's important someone be taught how to pick that wave otherwise it's useless. But I suppose many people try to surf on a vacation and never do it again. And I never did what Zach suggested – watch YouTube videos. Now I was paying for not having invested enough time in learning to surf.

Finally, I realized I had to try it. I couldn't just sit on the board for an hour and watch everyone. I also thought about the stories I could tell, the lies I could make up about how I did surf. Really, I couldn't do that either, even though no one would know.

I never made it up. I tried and fell right off the board several times. I was doing something wrong, I knew; it had just been a few weeks since I'd been in Australia. I felt a bit disappointed in myself.

But I reminded myself that it was my first time out there alone on the board. The fact that I'd rented the board and actually driven to the beach by myself to do this was more than I had planned for the trip. I needed this one day. There was still tomorrow.

Droves of teens seemed to be arriving for their surfing schools and although I had no idea what time it was, I also knew I had work to do. I unzipped the wetsuit halfway and carried the board back up the hill I had just come down.

"How you'd do?" Sam called from his spot on the couch when I arrived back at the house.

"I sucked the big egg," I said.

Still, I reminded myself of the good that had come from it. Another item on my list checked off. And the rest of that day I had a sense of, yes, I had gone out there and done it. I patted myself on the back, also grateful for spending that morning on the ocean. I wasn't afraid of it. I wasn't out deep enough for sharks (although I didn't ask either). I felt at home, like I belonged there. Things were coming together as they were supposed to.

*****

Friday was another day, not quite as sunny as Thursday but warm just the same. I don't think there was a cool spot anywhere in the country that July although after the oppressive heat of Chicago Los Angeles felt like a breeze.

Once again I carried the board down the paved hill, watching a surf school unload surfboards and hand them out to kids whose parents dropped them off. I felt envy, wishing I'd had a chance as a kid to experience that lifestyle. It had been a dream for me but it was part of their daily lives, especially in the summer. And like Jamie at the surf shop had said, the ocean is free. You don't have to pay to surf on it like you do to ski down a hill. Get a board and you're ready to go.

A mother was teaching her teenage son to my right and on my left a young girl was riding the waves with her dad. At first I thought she was much more experienced than me but then I saw that her dad was teaching her. Same with the mom; I thought she knew a lot about surfing. Turns out she was teaching herself and her son, having moved from Missouri to California the year before. So many assumptions, I realized. I thought I had "Novice" written in neon on a sign above my head. Some of them were no different than me, just trying to figure it out. Faking it until we figured it out.

This second day I knew I couldn't sit out there for very long. I had to get up on the board. I tried. I really did. I couldn't turn the board, with me on it, around quick enough, so I kept looking back at the waves. I knew it was the wrong way to do it but I had to figure this out and it seemed quicker that way.

I found myself picking waves that petered out. I would almost get up and then the wave would die. Or I'd land on the shore to find myself turning around to go back and being slammed against two more as I tried to move into them. Mostly I couldn't get turned around in time and ended up closer to the shoreline than before.

And one time I felt the board on top of me, something Merrick had warned me about. I felt it slide past over me. I didn't want to know how difficult surfing had been before the invention of ankle leashes, when people lost boards the way they now lose cell phone chargers.

Finally, I'd had enough. After a wave carried me all the way to the shore, I saw several more large ones crash in. What was I doing wrong? Why didn't I get this? And why couldn't I accept that I had done a lot in two days? Focus on the positive, I reminded myself, deciding I'd had enough, unzipping the wetsuit to my waist, and hiking the surfboard under my arm. As I trudged back up the hill, two older women came down and the first one asked, "How were the waves?"

"Oh, I didn't do so well," I admitted wondering if people told surfing stories as much as they told fishing stories.

"What happened?" she asked, acting as if she thought I had gotten hurt.

"I'm okay," I reassured her. "I couldn't pick the waves, though. I thought I picked a good one and then two better ones would come after it."

"Just like husbands," her friend said, waving at me.

I couldn't stop laughing, forgetting what I was carrying under my arm up the hill.

Carrying the board wasn't bad. Although it's bulky, especially for a short person like me, it almost feels like a badge of honor. Hey look: I'm a surfer! I sucked today but I've been up on a board. And knowing how many people will never try, I do feel pretty good about that since I never thought I'd even have the opportunity.

5

It wasn't until after I finished attempting to surf the second time that I realized how much surfing epitomized my life that at that moment. My life had been filled with change and transition for almost a year. I had felt it coming for several years, more with my career than with my personal life, but I was in the midst of it on those days when I carried that surfboard down to the ocean under my arm.

I was nervous about going out on the ocean on my own, just as I was nervous about life planting me back on my own in many ways. But on the ocean I wasn't nervous. I felt very at home riding the board, whether sitting on it, lying on it, or, when I found the right wave, standing on it. I thought it would be scary and hard to balance, but I was learning that it would take time to master the technical side. I had never been involved in sports that had technical sides. When I was running in high school, there wasn't much to it compared to today. They sent us out to the door and told us how long to run. On the track it was either a tempo run or go at it hard. It depended on the day during the season. We didn't have fabrics that "wicked away" our sweat or a million road races to pick from.

While surfing still remains primitive in many ways, thank goodness, for the first time in my life I find that I'm intrigued by this technical piece. Maybe it's because I have the patience for the first time in my life, just as I picked up knitting very easily not long after surfing in Hawaii. Or maybe it was just time.

I'm ready for new ventures, although surfing is an old one rekindled. A stick figure on a board graces my car, making it easy for me to find my not-so-unusual white SUV. The hardest part is that I want it to come more easily. Everyone thinks I'm a better surfer than I am. "You're a pro now, right?" my friend Chris teased me. I admit I'm not very good, but I also know that I will stick with it until I get better. I want to get better. Yes, I can say I'm a surfer because I've been up on a board, but I want to say that I do more than that. And I will.

My life is moving along the same way. It's not coming along as fast as I would like. I moved a year ago, and there are some things I'd like to progress further. Then I remind myself that some of them I can't control. I have to let them go and find others to focus on. Just like on the ocean, I have to ride a few waves before I find ones worthy of attempting to stand up on.

Patience. I'm being taught patience on the board and in my life. I'm more patient on the board now. Something tells me it will come. "You need to do it for two weeks straight and you'll get it," Jamie told me when we returned the board. "I was terrible when I started."

After all, life is about the journey, not the destination. Yeah, yeah, I don't believe that all the time either. I just keep repeating it. However, I do know that many times I've understood it when I've accomplished something. Whether it be a newly published book in my hand, "Pomp and Circumstance" playing as I walked across the stage for a diploma, or a finished knit scarf, I remember all it took to get to that moment. Life is about those smaller moments, not about the big ones.

I always tell people that as they struggle with their grief, life isn't about the big, happy moments— the holidays, the vacations—it's about those everyday routine events that we sometimes don't appreciate until they are gone: the cups of coffee shared with a loved one over the morning newspaper and the sun shining through the trees in our backyard.

For me, those two days on the ocean were not just about getting up on the board but also about the time I spent on the ocean, being present in my life. There was no time for daydreaming when I needed to watch for waves I wanted to catch.

6

No one really knows what is going on in other people's lives. Several times people have told me that they are surprised that I have difficulties to cope with. My life is no different than anyone else's. What might be different is how I choose to handle those trying times.

I know what it's like to not want to get out of bed in the morning or cope with the day. However, I have a long list of things to do most days. I have dogs who need to be fed. I have a run I'm expecting myself to do. I might walk part of it but it's still important that I get out and do it.

No matter how bad I'm feeling, though, or how much it might feel like life is against me, there is always hope in the sunrise. When we feel bad, darkness is the worst, the most difficult part of the day. My thoughts in darkness often dissipate when the light comes.

For the seventeen years I lived in Albuquerque, but mostly in the second half of those years, I ran before the sun came up. By the time I took Chaco out for his run, the sun would be emerging from behind the Sandia Mountains. It was an incredible sight each morning, one that I never tired of. And on mornings where clouds lingered, the sky turned pink and orange. How could I not feel hopeful seeing that?

I draw strength from the sun, even long before it's high enough in the sky to warm my skin. It feels as if the new day is like a freshly washed chalkboard. It's a clean slate to start a new day, and with a new day, we never know what will happen. A friend once said that things can change quickly. While we could be feeling down one moment, a phone call or something unexpectedly good could come out of the blue and turn our day, and even life, around. Miracles, she said. We are surrounded by miracles waiting to happen.

We all have symbols of hope in our lives, things that keep us going.

Talking about suicide, grief, and loss doesn't make me sad. It doesn't bring me down. It doesn't make me want to kill myself. What it does is the opposite. It makes me feel hopeful because it connects me to people. As it's a topic that most people are uncomfortable discussing, when I do talk with people about it, they usually open up about their own experiences. And their own experience isn't always negative. Sometimes they have learned something from it or have something they can use to help others. In those moments, I get a lot of hope, and it's hope that I can usually share with others.

*****

Maria Shriver said in a *Newsweek* essay that she knows our power in life isn't about our resume. Instead it's about being true to ourselves and finding our own voices and paths in the world.

We all have the opportunity to be our authentic selves. My friend Chris tells me, when I'm feeling frustrated that things aren't moving as quickly as I would like in selling books or picking up speaking engagements, that I need to continue to be who I'm supposed to be and it will fall together.

The more we are our authentic selves, the better our lives will be. It means life will take us on the most rewarding path. I often think of the people I knew when I was growing up, particularly in high school, who pretended to be someone they weren't. Granted, it's all about growing up and sometimes we have to travel these roads to find who we are, but those experiences never lead us very far. As we continue to travel through adulthood, I see people I know who have changed so much about themselves or sold out in some way. They have strayed from their true selves. And I know that while I might be frustrated that my messages are slower to getting to the mass audience, I also realize that being true to who I am will take me further in life and will pay off in the long run.

Part V

1

I hadn't dreamt about my sister Denise in a long time. Even so, I didn't remember much about this particular dream. Except for one thing: her death hadn't been a suicide but a homicide or an accident. The sense of peace that I felt when I woke up that morning told me it didn't matter which because it was the message that was important: The suicide didn't exist anymore. It didn't define me, and it didn't define her. I saw it as a message that I was off the road of suicide grief. I had completed whatever I needed to do, and now it was time to move on.

Why did I have the dream that night? My life was changing. The day before I had the dream had been packed with events around other parts of my life. I had visited the priest at church to discuss a book I was thinking about writing (not this one although we did talk about it). In the days immediately preceding the dream and following it I was preparing to leave for another trip to Southern California to pick up the surfboard Jamie the surf shop owner had shaped for me, and to spend two weeks there surfing and writing.

Several days before the dream, it was as if someone placed a billboard in front of me and gave me a huge message: much of my life had been on hold since Denise's death. I never would have said that before but a freelance gig with *The Naperville Sun*, my hometown newspaper, opened my eyes.

I'd answered a Facebook message looking for freelance writers to cover various beats. I had a history with the newspaper; when we were growing up it was the place we saw our names when we got varsity letters, made honor rolls, or appeared in pictures of school events. When we graduated from high school, my classmate Stephanie and I had won the *Sun's* college journalism scholarships and our photo appeared in the newspaper with then-owner Harold White. The summer after my sophomore year I had an opportunity to write for the newspaper, but it didn't work out and I went on with my life. I found out later from my sister Denise, whose best friend's mother worked at the paper, that the reason I hadn't been hired was because I didn't have a driver's license.

I'd taken driver's education at fifteen and hated driving. Every year I renewed the blue slip, my ticket that I was eligible to take the test, and every year I didn't take the test. My sister Karen took me to the MetLife building parking lot and I drove in so many circles that she felt sick (reading the newspaper while I was driving wasn't a good idea).

Hoping to motivate me, my friend Laura gave me a keychain with my name painted on it. My sister Denise learned to drive, and I let her cart us around, mostly to places like Cub Foods so we could buy Kemp's strawberry frozen yogurt and Archway oatmeal cookies to make frozen yogurt sandwiches while we watched the late Cubs-Dodgers game from Los Angeles on the black-and white-television in the kitchen.

After my college graduation and before I moved to Albuquerque for graduate school, a year after Denise's death, I finally tackled the test and passed.

I never thought that I would write for *The Naperville Sun* after that. I had different interests by then and I didn't plan to move back to Naperville. Yet there I was signing the contract for a weekly column about people who work for good causes, people like me who have a passion for making a difference.

When I came out of the *Sun's* office that afternoon, the billboard popped up in front of me. I had circled around to where I'd left off in 1993. I never saw it in 1993, probably because I was a busy college student. And when Denise died, it was all about coping with the loss and integrating it into my life.

But I now saw how many things had simply stopped in the years before Denise died. They weren't obvious; life just seemed to change, and that's not unusual, especially when we are in our late teens and early twenties. Surfing didn't feel so important. I didn't think about moving to Los Angeles, especially after life moved me to New Mexico. My focus became Colorado, thanks to the summer at the Olympic Training Center. I never made it to Los Angeles and I often joked that I planned to go to LA at one time but only made it as far as New Mexico, as if the car broke down there and I never left. I had a neighbor who told me that had happened to them: in the 1950s they were moving from rural Kansas to Los Angeles when their car broke down in Albuquerque and they didn't have the money to fix it. Her then-husband found a job there and they never left or looked back. I saw my life much the same way.

None of it was bad. It was life, and life had changed. It's hard for me to imagine how I would have changed if Denise hadn't died because I was so young when it happened. I had never spent much time thinking about, it but that week, after signing the contract with the newspaper, the billboard was hard to miss.

Running, too, had changed in my life. For many years I ran just a few miles a day. Some days I walked a bit. But now I didn't feel the need to push myself anymore. I thought it was because of my age, and it didn't bother me. I was content to run a few miles and then run-walk the four dogs. But around the time I felt suicide and grief drifting out of my life, running seemed to be pushing back in. I started to run more miles. Then I began to run harder. I bought a slew of new running clothes, for the first time enjoying all the dry-fit and sweat-wicking fabrics. I couldn't quite figure out my reasons for running hard, but something told me it would come and to continue to work on building up where I was at.

I saw how the road of my life had come to an end and I'd gone on a different road. It was as if life had prepared me for Denise's death with these changes. I wouldn't have time to focus on many of them and life knew that. I had to work through my grief and it would then take me on a road to helping others. When Denise died, I never would have said my life ended. I know people say that but it never felt that way with me. Life kept going and I had a choice whether to be part of it or not.

While for a long time I felt that because of her death the world was no longer my oyster, somewhere inside of me the Michelle I wanted to be and the goals I wanted to accomplish were still cooking. I had put aside the cross-country manuscript, but it was still there, sitting on the floor by my desk. The things that were important to me remained in my life in small ways but not until I closed in on the twentieth anniversary of Denise's death did they re-emerge.

I had returned to where I'd left off in 1993, although I had become in many ways a different person. The opportunities coming to me were the ones I thought I'd left behind. I could feel the road ending and merging back with the one I left. I liked it. I felt like the woman I wanted to be all those years ago. I could look in the mirror and be happy with the person looking back at me. I was more me than at any other time in my life. And I was happy with that.

2

Sam and Lois invited me back. Jamie offered to shape a board. I figured it was the perfect opportunity to see if I could really learn to surf and decided to go for it.

I first spent time with Sam and Lois in the fall of 2008 when I spoke at Loyola Marymount University. Our dog Daisy was dying of hemangiosarcoma, an evil terminal cancer of the blood vessels, and Joe was managing her care in Albuquerque while I was away. I sat in their car, having arrived back at the house after my talk, in the driveway, because my cell phone didn't work in the house. Most of the time I was lucky if it worked across the street.

They were kind enough to let me stay and spend a few days with them in Palos Verdes, where they have lived since 1967. Their son Sammy died by suicide in 1982. I had no idea in 2008 it would be the first of several trips I would make to see them and visit Los Angeles. I also spent my fortieth birthday weekend at their house, leaving late the morning of my birthday to see other friends and spend the night in San Diego with yet other friends.

Before staying at their house, I didn't know Sam and Lois as well as some of my other fellow suicide survivors. Everyone loves Sam and Lois, though. I remembered them from my first American Association of Suicidology Conference, held in Los Angeles in 2000, the conference that would ultimately bring me into the AAS fold and alter my life in many ways. I never talked to them at the conference, only saw them in passing, as they were the co-chairs of the Healing After Suicide Conference.

Many people tell stories of losing friends after a suicide. Sometimes it's because of fear, sometimes it's because they don't know what to say. I was lucky when my sister died. I had great friends who continued to be there for me. There were few who disappeared off my radar. Friends would drift out of my life over the years but I don't believe it was due to the death of Denise. It was just life. I have several friends who were there for me then and whom I still count as good friends today.

I always tell people that any friends they lose in that time, they will replace with more meaningful friends along the grief road. Sometimes we become friends with people on the grief road who are only with us a short time. I often say that the scenery changes along the road and so do some of the people who walk with us.

For me though, the number of friends I have seems to have multiplied because of my work in the grief and loss field. I also have noticed that these friends are more meaningful to my life. There are other people who were part of my life when Denise died and are still somewhat in my life, but I don't feel a connection to them like I once did. While some of this might be life, I believe it also has to do with the fact that we don't tolerate a lot of meaninglessness in our lives after the loss. We want a deeper connection to people.

What I appreciate about Sam and Lois, besides their kindness to me and letting me store my surfboard in their garage, is that their marriage has lasted sixty-some years. Looking at some of the couples who lost children to suicide and became pioneers in the movement for the suicide bereaved, I have seen some of the strongest marriages ever. LaRita and Eldon Archibald, my friends in Colorado Springs, are another remarkable couple with an amazingly long-lived marriage.

To listen to Sam and Lois kid each other, mostly Sam kidding Lois, especially after they got a rescue dog named Rocky between my last visits, cracked me up. "Your friend Lois," Sam would say to me "She has to buy the most expensive treats for the dog."

But it also gave me hope, looking at all they had been through and how they had been able to pull together. Just as my family talks about Denise and our memories of her, the Blooms talk about Sammy and their years with him. Sammy and Denise might not be here today but they remain part of our families, and that helps us continue to move forward. We realize that we can move on because they are still with us and no one can take our memories away.

Seeing Sam and Lois though, also gives me hope that there is a lasting relationship out there for me. I still believe in the fairy-tale ending, that we all should have someone in our lives whom we can rely on. I know what that's like because I had it once, and I hope to have it again. Watching them tease each other, even after more than sixty years together, and seeing they still have things to talk about after sixty years, brings me a lot of happiness.

3

"That's the first thing you want to see in the morning," Ethan said sarcastically, when we parked in the lot by Rat Beach, pointing at two elderly men in Speedo swimming suits toweling off after a swim in the ocean. I knew then I liked Ethan. He reminded me of Zach, the curly-haired first teacher I had in New Hampshire. And in many ways they were the same, both around twenty, both in college, both involved in other activities (BMX racing for Zach, paintball competition for Ethan), and obviously they both loved to surf.

I hadn't planned on taking more lessons. My friend Chris kept suggesting that I took too many and just needed to go out into the ocean and surf. But I knew this was the best way for me to start my two weeks in Palos Verdes. If I was going to surf each day, at least I could start out with as much help as possible. It definitely wouldn't hurt.

The day before I had picked up my new board, Sam and Lois going with me for what I called a "family outing." I never in my life thought I would own a surfboard, but here was mine sitting next to me on its side in Lois and Sam's minivan as I drove to meet Ethan. Even better, Jamie had shaped the board just for me. Using my height, weight, skill level, and the lessons he's learned about shaping boards over the years, it was customized for me. It was white with an orange rim, orange being my favorite color because of the energy it brings.

Ethan waxed the board, explaining that the wax would stick my feet to the board (Sam later joked that he never understood why people couldn't just wax their feet instead). For the first time in my life I owned board wax. It sounds silly that it made me giddy, but these were things I read about in magazines, saw in stores, but had never been part of my life. All I'd had was my Catch It T-shirt, board shorts, and the photos posted on my walls from that surfing magazine I'd bought on my trip to Florida in high school.

Ethan also told me how he'd lost a front tooth surfing and gotten stitches in his leg from getting tangled up with the fins of his board. These experiences I didn't want to admit I wasn't ready for, although he did acknowledge his favorite way to surf was in the fog, a time when he said you can't see any other surfers in the lineup, making you feel as if you are alone on the ocean. While I admit that I am more scared of sending my bicycle flying down my steep driveway (with me riding it) than I am of surfing a wave, I also am not ready for the kinds of waves Ethan thrives on.

The waves were small when we approached the ocean, and that was fine by me. I felt patient by then. Ethan told me he'd learned the hard way that he didn't control the ocean, often begging it to bring him the big waves. I'm sure I would have been that way at his age, too. Now it meant something different to me. Zach had told me older people like me were much better surfing students because egos weren't involved.

There was still much for me to learn about the ocean, and my misconceptions about surfing were endless. All my life, I had thought it was about getting up on the board. If you could that, you were a surfer. I'd done it fairly easily in New Hampshire. But I'd also done it with Zach pushing the board behind me and calling out to me when to stand up.

The reality is that surfing is much more than that. While for most people a lesson is about standing up on the board and being able to go home from a vacation to tell one's friends, "Hey, I got up on a surfboard! I'm a surfer!" to me it was about learning something else. You can't go out and surf the big waves from the beginning. Just like life being about the journey rather than the destination, surfing is about continued understanding, respecting, and learning the ocean. I knew none of that when I started, but Ethan taught me what I needed to know.

I had no regrets about the time I'd spent not getting up on the board three weeks before on my last trip to Southern California. I asked Ethan about all of it and he helped me see what I'd done wrong and why. He taught me that waves come in sets although these are never predictable because the ocean isn't predictable. Sometimes, he explained, the best waves come behind one that looks great. All of those things make surfing magical because we never know what's next. It also makes it hard to leave the water.

As I lay on my board, we watched waves and dodged an influx of seaweed. He explained that was part of an incoming swell. He pointed at waves in the distance, showing me how the ones that show some breaking off in the distance are the good waves. I began to point at them and ask, "That's a good one?" bound and determined to learn how to do this. I was going to be on my own out there for almost two weeks, and I was going to be up on the board. I knew that when I got back from my trip on the ocean with my virgin board, everyone would want to know if I'd gotten up on the board. That was the myth of what was important. I knew better, but how did I explain that to everyone else?

"I'm glad you're interested in understanding about surfing," Ethan said, answering all my questions, probably happy to share his own knowledge of something that he called his religion. I was just grateful someone was willing to share this knowledge with me.

We couldn't stay out there forever, though, having our conversation with the water. I needed to get up on the board. Ethan told me earlier, in a nice way, that my paddling was lazy and then explained how when he was in his early teens he hung out with the high school surfers and they battered him in ways that made him made better, forcing him to paddle into the biggest waves, which in turn helped his strength and lessened any fear he had of the waves.

Ethan taught me how to push up off the board before a big wave came, to separate myself from the board and allow the wave to go between us. And then there was the "turtle": flipping off the board and under it when a big wave comes.

I also began to let go of how I looked. I will be the first person to admit how vain I can be. I will change my clothes if a see a spot on something I'm wearing, and I will choose being stylish over being warm.

Jamie had already told me that the weather was so warm that people weren't wearing wet suits while surfing. Ethan told me he'd be wearing one even though he also admitted he would be sweating in it. I brought my shorty wet suit with me, brand new out of the box from Amazon, but chose the bikini bottoms with a rash guard on top. However, when we got down to the water and I saw a sea of black floating on boards, I wondered if I had made the right choice. Turned out only my forearms were cold, the one place in my body I have been chronically cold since I lost weight as a serious runner in high school.

I had always been aware of having that slicked back hair look, and in my time surfing by myself, I spent a lot of time trying to fix my hair that way and make it look good, even though when I saw photos of myself wearing that look, I never liked them. Somehow it made me feel more glamorous. As I tumbled through the waves, Ethan calling out to me when I came up for air, asking me if I was okay, I would call back fine. And I was. That's when I let go of slicking back the hair. Although it was ponytailed in the back, the front still went where it wanted, and I decided I didn't care. I would rather paddle back to the wave than think about my hair.

The first wave he sent me out into died before I got up. Those perfect waves we hear about are few and far between. A lot of surfing is sitting out on the ocean waiting. And waiting. And waiting more.

Sitting out there, I lose all sense of time. Other surfers say the same thing happens to them. Being out there with Ethan, and the others I'd taken lessons from, gave me an opportunity to share that time with someone else, and when I was out alone I did wish someone was there to share it with me. But I also know that it's a time to forget about what's happening beyond where the shore breaks, beyond the sand, beyond the road that leads to the ocean. It's out there on the water looking for a wave that has those cracks on the top, where we're in the present. I had writing to do when I got back to the house but as long as I was on the water, I told myself that I wasn't going to think about it. My writing would still be there when I got back. I fell off another time, going up too late and missing the momentum of the wave itself. The next wave I missed, going up too late again, this time the arches of my feet not centered to the middle of the board (obvious by the line Jamie had strategically placed in it). I promptly fell off. "You went up just fraction of a second too late," Ethan told me when we met back up.

I knew we were nearing the end of our time together, and I knew I had to get up on the board. I didn't make it up on the next one either. The time between the waves and sets seemed to be getting longer. I almost got up on this one but it sent me sailing into the water and I somersaulted forward, probably the only time in my life I've somersaulted in the ocean without touching the ocean floor.

"That one broke too early," Ethan said. "It wasn't your fault."

When the next wave came, I waited for him to call out when to go up, and I didn't hear him. Maybe I missed it in the wave. The ocean was pulling me forward, but I knew I was running out of ocean before the shore. I popped up and almost made it.

We had time for one more. I didn't think about the fact that everyone was going to ask me if I'd gotten up. I didn't care. Ethan had taught me what I needed to know to go out on my own for the next two weeks. When I popped up, it felt right. I had it. And then I fell off. But for the first time that day it felt right. I needed to practice. Like riding a bike, Ethan said, one day I wouldn't even think about the placement of my feet on the board.

While I floated out on the ocean on my board, Ethan treading water next to me, I thought about the strength of the water. I didn't feel scared of it, even when Ethan warned me of the stingrays that he and his girlfriend had encountered the week before. "Shuffle your feet on the ocean floor," he said, "Remember, we're coming into their territory." Respect for the ocean was important. I felt comfortable out there, but I realized you can't forget the strength of the ocean. You have to respect it or it will remind you when it sends you flying through a huge wave as you're trying to work your way back to where you can catch another wave.

Life is just the same. We can't take it for granted. It's stronger than us, and if we don't respect it each day, each moment that we are present in it, it will get the best of us. So much about the conversation with the water amounts to understanding how the water and surfing are like life. Just as running had provided me with the skills to help me cope with my grief, surfing was providing me with the skills to move forward with my life beyond grief, suicide, loss, and every other skin I was ready to shed.

It wasn't until we were walking back up the hill, Ethan carrying my board, that he asked me what I spoke about in my public appearances. When I told him, I quickly saw that he had something he wanted to say. It wasn't what I expected.

He began to recount how his grandmother had been the person to raise him, how she had been the one who took him to the ocean on dark mornings so he could surf before school. How she had died a year ago. He'd met "the girl of his dreams" shortly after and he admitted there was a struggle.

"She can't be the love that my grandmother gave me," he said, smoking a cigarette as we drove down the Pacific Coast Highway back to the surf shop. "But I also know she is struggling to be independent at twenty-one."

I had called the surf shop several times earlier that week, my Type A personality needing to check in on my board. It had been Ethan who had answered. The person I was talking to now was far from the surfer boy who had answered the phone.

I was twenty-one when Denise died. Life wreaked havoc on my romantic relationships. Ethan and I were very much alike in this respect. I heard once that we can only do so much inner work alone, that someone must journey with us to truly help us heal from the hurts in life.

This is easier said than done. In my own life, I saw that I would rather work at accomplishing my goals. It was less hurtful because I was the only one to blame for anything. Life has changed me and I understand that life isn't meant to be experienced alone. We can be independent but we also can be part of a duo.

I'm not sure who taught each other more that morning on the ocean.

4

Loss is energy consuming but it offers us an opportunity to make ourselves better. Each time something happens to me, no matter how small or large the loss looms, I use it to ask myself how I can be better for the future. It's not easy to see, but our relationships always show us ways we can be better people. When we look at what frustrated us about someone and the relationship, we should ask ourselves, What can I do better? By turning the question on ourselves, we have the opportunity to become better for the next relationship. I don't believe that the end of any marriage or relationship is one-sided. Each person played a part and played some parts better than others. When my marriage ended, my goal became to work on how I could be better for what and who comes next for me.

It was no coincidence that my marriage ended just when my career took its sharpest turn. I clung to the work in the suicide and grief field partly because I needed the money but also because I didn't know what else I was going to do. When I moved to Chicago, I still didn't know what I was going to do, but I had a profound sense of finally feeling able to let go of a number of projects that kept me aligned with work in suicide and grief.

The end of a marriage is also a reminder that life is about love. I had denied this for a long time. Because of various things that had happened to me, I began to believe that my life wasn't about love in any way, that I would never have that love that I saw some of my friends have with their spouses and their children. And when I was labeled single again by a judge's signature, I found myself looking at families in various places—church, restaurants, in my neighborhood— and thinking how great they had it. I'm sure they had difficulties but I could also see how a group of people truly cared about each other, and I was sad not to be part of a partnership anymore.

I also began to wear pink. I wouldn't say that pink was ever my favorite color. Yes, I had a pink plastic bucket and I loved the Barbie aisle of any store, but I didn't wear too much pink. In the years after I finished graduate school, pink was not a color you were caught wearing if you wanted to be taken seriously. In sports journalism I would have been laughed at, and in the classroom it was hard enough getting taken seriously as a short blonde woman. That began to change in the years leading up to 2012, and I found myself wanting to wear pink again and feeling good about it. Then I found out pink is the color of love. I know, I know, why didn't I realize that before? Like I said, I didn't think my life was about love.

5

I long ago settled my only regret after Denise's death. I have known people who never let their regrets go and let them dictate their entire lives. I have few in my life because I always try to take them and think what I can do in the future to make sure I don't feel that way again.

With Denise's death though, my only regret was that I never told her I loved her. We often talked about how the word "love" is overused, so when we wrote each other letters in those last few years of her life when I was away at college, we ended them with "always." Anyone can say they love someone, we reasoned, but there were other ways to show it that meant more.

Denise went on a church retreat about two years before her death and wrote me a letter telling me that she loved me. She said she did it because she knew it was something we never said to each other. However, I never reciprocated, and her death left me without the opportunity to tell her that.

Compared to the guilt that many people feel after a suicide, what I felt was very insignificant, because it didn't take me long to realize that she knew I loved her. She didn't doubt that, just as I never doubted she loved me. After all, her death wasn't about me. She couldn't see beyond about two feet in front of her. It was as if she built a brick wall in front of herself and couldn't feel the love that any of us had for her. She was too embroiled in disliking herself. I also knew that my love would not have saved her. What caused her to end her life was what she felt inside, and none of us could have changed that.

I know Denise knows that I continue to love her because she is still present in my life. She's still my biggest cheerleader and part of who I continue to become.

Learning that life is about love has been harder for me, though.

I became jaded at various points in my life. My experiences made me suspicious of love. I felt that I had to be independent, and love has an element of dependence to it. I began to think that life wasn't about love and instead, for me, maybe it was about my career. That wasn't a bad thing, I reasoned. I do have people in my life that I love and who love me, but maybe romantic love isn't for everyone.

My marriage wasn't ripped away from me nor was my relationship with Joe. It leaked out over a period of time. And when it was gone, when I found myself alone, which wasn't bad, part of me began to see that maybe there was something I was missing. Could I love someone without feeling dependent? That was what I had to learn.

6

I never thought that surfing was about patience. I thought you got out on the ocean and you caught wave after wave after wave. While I knew during the lessons I took that not all waves are created equal, I also learned that there is a lot of waiting that happens between the waves worth surfing. Ethan had taught me how to choose waves, and I found that I wasn't hopeless at choosing them. I wasn't necessarily doing anything wrong. But the next morning, a Saturday, when I went back to Rat Beach by myself, I continued to assume that everyone else knew more about surfing than I did.

For the first time in my surfing experience, about half the surfers were female that day. Although I look younger than forty, I knew this group was younger than me, and I admit I was envious because they probably grew up surfing. And, again, I assumed they knew more than me. There was another surprise on the waves: about a fourth of the men were, well, not very young. Again, I was envious knowing that all these people spent a lot of time on the waves.

I paddled out to the lineup and did some wave watching but also people watching. The two guys on my right were discussing a baby and then something about going to IKEA to put something together. Two Asian-looking girls sat on their boards together and I imagined they were catching up on life activities. Everyone chose different waves, though. There was no wave that each person took. Even the two guys next to me didn't surf the same waves. One went at one time; the other would wait until later.

They didn't all get up and surf either. It made me realize that they weren't any different from me. I had to get over my fear of being a novice and just do it. I tried to surf more waves than the previous day or the days three weeks ago but found my timing was off. It was okay. I was getting better at picking the waves, and eventually I would catch them in time. I still struggled with turning around fast enough, and I found it hard to sit on the back of my board, but again, I know that will come. I was still comfortable out there and it was nice to know I was using my own surfboard.

There is an incredible amount of patience that comes with surfing. Just like life, just like grief. We don't have all the control that we think we do, and we have to learn to trust that it will all work out. Some people try to control their grief, just as Ethan told me he tried to control the ocean, begging it to bring him a good wave.

I don't like the phrase that "time heals all wounds" but to some extent time is an important factor in grief. In time our perspective changes, our grief doesn't feel so sharp, and we are able to focus. Of course we also must be engaged with life, not sitting on the side of the road watching everyone go by. In that same sense, I can't just sit on my surfboard and not do anything. I have to be patient for the right waves but I also need to make an effort to ride them when they look like they are worth riding.

Sometimes it's hard to be patient, especially when we want something to happen. I find my biggest problem in surfing is that I let my mind wander. I'm not at that point yet where I can focus on anything but watching the waves, selecting the right one, and turning around and paddling before it gets to me. When I let my mind wander, I miss it. In the same way, if we ignore grief or we let life pass us by, we are missing out on opportunities to learn more about who we are and to become stronger people. There's a balancing act of being patient and also taking opportunities that help us grow.

I could easily have never gotten up on a surfboard. I never had to take that lesson back in New Hampshire. I never had to ask Pua or Jill for help to go surfing in Hawaii or Australia. And I never had to mention surfing to Lois and Sam. I could easily have stayed in my box. However, had I done that I would have missed so many opportunities to learn. I couldn't write this book. I wouldn't have learned from the ocean, from the people who have taught me so much about it and life.

There are many things I have done in my life that I didn't have to do. After my sister died, I could have chosen to do nothing. I didn't have to write the book for sibling survivors of suicide, I didn't have to tell her story to people around the world or to the media. I could have kept it to myself. But had I done that, I never would have had the experiences that I've had. Some days I want to stay in my box. I have been part of events that forced me out of my box right after people close to me in my life have died. And some days—well, we all have them. We don't want to try something new. But I grew in those times and I became confident because of them. I wouldn't be who I am without those experiences.

But I've also had to be patient when things aren't moving as quickly as I would like. Anyone who knows me is probably laughing at the very idea that I can be patient because they know I want to control things, I want them to move faster, I want so much to happen. When I started my doctoral program, a wise friend told me to slow down. My focus was on the dissertation, but he reminded me that it was about the journey and to enjoy the coursework and everything that would lead to that dissertation. Had I not done that, I would have missed out on so much that I was able to turn into other writings and talks that helped others. I was able to bridge the gap in the suicide grief world where we weren't talking about the family as a unit. We'd become too focused on the individual relationships in the family. It was my coursework, the journey, that opened my eyes to this new approach.

7

For a long time after the deaths of loved ones, the people left behind were told to sever the attachment because the loved one was no longer part of their lives. I feel fortunate to live in a time where this approach has gone out of fashion. It certainly wasn't the case with the losses in my life. In workshops and talks I often told people that the bond wasn't broken; instead it was changed. I point out that one of the difficult parts of loss is that change from the person being in our physical world to being with us in a different way. I don't believe that time comes into play in this change, because it's not a passive process. If time alone allowed everyone to heal from any sort of loss, then the only hurting people in the world would be those who are coping with a recent loss. Grief is a process where we learn about ourselves but also learn how to let our loved ones be with us in a different way.

Denise had given a talk in her advanced speech class about the rodeo, and she started the speech by singing part of the Garth Brooks song "Rodeo." This is the one video recording we have of her, and for me it became the sign that she was with me. It was easy because at the time I listened to country music and the song came on the radio more often. However, there were other times later on when it would pop up on the radio, maybe when I was in a rental car trying to find good music on an unfamiliar radio dial.

After my dad died though, I often forgot that Denise was with me. I no longer needed to think about her as much. I talked about her so often talks that I knew she was with me. It wasn't like surfing where I hadn't mastered everything yet; it was second nature like surfing is for people who have been doing it for years. I didn't need to focus on her now. She was with me and I didn't doubt that.

Not until a year after my dad died, though, did I begin to get a sense of him being with me. This took longer for some reason. I'm sure it was because I was at a different stage in my life and his death was different. Sometimes I also believe it was because there was such a long period of time between their deaths.

I didn't get it at first, but he began to leave coins. I had never found coins anywhere, and then I started to find them. I might have found a few and not realized what they were, but in the Orlando Airport I saw a coin under my chair when we were going home at the end of a vacation and it occurred to me that it was from Dad.

His life revolved around money. He was notorious for leaving change everywhere—on the coffee table, on the kitchen counter. Wherever Dad had been, there were always coins lying around. People I told thought that I had trained my eyes to find them but I never found them when I was looking for them. Sometimes they came during difficult times and I saw the coins as reminders that, despite what I was going through, Dad was letting me know he was with me.

At times I would find multiple coins in a week. Sometimes it wasn't just pennies. One morning on a run I found two one-dollar bills and an unlit cigarette in the street. At first I was grossed out by the cigarette but then laughed when I realized it was my dad "the smoker."

As the years went by, the coins would continue to come, and people would often tell me that they found coins and thought of me. It was great they thought of me, but I was sure that it was their own loved ones sending them signs. Perhaps I was the one who opened them up to the possibility. Sometimes I found a 1975 penny, the year that Denise was born. I always thought that was the sign that both Dad and Denise were with me.

In the past year though, I felt a change with Denise. I got very caught up in all the signs from Dad, and it felt like Denise was on the back burner, but again, it was because I didn't need a sign that she was with me. I knew she was there. For a long time it would send me to tears when I heard any of the songs from her funeral played in church– "On Eagle's Wings," "Be Not Afraid," and "Amazing Grace."

However, I didn't attribute those songs to her being with me until one Saturday evening Mass when I was with a man with whom I was going to spend some time afterward. "Be Not Afraid" came on and sent me crying. My friend had gotten up to blow his nose, his allergies getting the best of him, getting away during the song so he didn't miss anything.

In that moment it was as if Denise knocked me in the head to remind me that she too was still in my life. My sister had always been positive that one day I would have a man in my life, one with whom I would truly be happy. In the years before her death she watched several not work out, and I think it disappointed her as much as it disappointed me. For Christmas my freshman year of college, she gave me two glasses from Marshall Field's with Christmas trees on them. When I looked at her strangely, she said, "For one day when you have someone in your life."

I held onto those glasses for years, and while I don't have them now, I did make this a scene in *Sisters: The Karma Twist*. That night in church Denise was reminding me she was there with me and wishing that my friend and I would have a great time together.

I know now that she comes to me in more than just those few songs. Recently, I have started to ask her to bring me a good song when I'm out for a run, and she usually follows through. Sometimes even the song titles have meaning. I was frustrated with someone and mumbled under my breath on my run that it was going to be the day I made someone make a decision about something and then next song on my iPod Shuffle was "Moment of Truth" by Survivor. I almost had to stop running because I was laughing so hard.

Our loved ones who have died are with us if we allow them to show us their presence in our lives. I know that my dad continues to come to me because each time I find a coin I thank him. If I kept walking by the coins or not acknowledging them, they would stop. He would have given up.

It helps to know that they are still with me. It makes the pain that they are not in my physical life less sharp. While I can't carry on a conversation with them as I did when they were alive, they are still experiencing life events with me and they are helping me to find happiness and hope on the journey.

8

Sometimes we have to be careful what thoughts cross our minds. As I drove to the ocean on a Sunday morning, I kept wishing I wasn't going surfing alone. While I am accustomed to doing things on my own and don't mind it, for some reason I felt like surfing was something to be shared—maybe not all the time, but sometimes. And, like fish stories, it's proof that you actually caught a wave. I know that it's not about what I share with everyone so much as what it means to me and how it feels to catch the wave but Sam did tell me jokingly, as I walked out the door, not to return unless I stood on the board.

I admitted to him I was a bit concerned there would be too many people in the lineup. "It's not that I care what they think of me falling off my board," I said, having finally gotten over that. "I'm more afraid of colliding with someone because I don't feel I have great control of the board yet."

Tomorrow, I said would be the day I'd get up.

But driving down the hill from their house to the beach, I thought about how it would be good to be surfing with someone else, simply so that someone could tell me what I was missing or doing wrong. In my mind, I had to be doing something wrong since I couldn't get up on the board. But I also knew it would come. I had felt it when it was right: how balanced you feel on the board, and how that feels easy and you know that you might be on top of the waves but you're doing it, you're surfing.

When I reached the parking lot, I saw Ethan with someone, probably giving a lesson. I figured I would catch up with him down below. But I wasn't prepared for what came next. A man about my age pulled up facing me and asked me how the waves were.

"I haven't gone out yet," I said, placing the minivan key in the handy-dandy leash key pocket (I could kiss the person who invented that and Ethan for showing it to me).

We struck up a conversation and walked down to the beach together, passing Ethan and his student. "If you go to the second lifeguard stand," Scott said, pointing, "the waves are better." I hadn't planned to follow Scott but I kept going. "And I know some people out here. They'll let you have the good waves."

There were fewer people out that morning and no women, unlike the day before. Scott introduced me to his friend Fred, and I found myself among the local surfing community for the first time.

I tried to explain I was new at surfing. They had been surfing since they were in their teens, and they were older than me (but they were also shocked that I was forty, and not in my twenties like they thought I was). I didn't mind being a novice; more than anything I just didn't want anyone to treat me badly because of that. This probably stems from having to work so hard being a woman covering men's intercollegiate sports in college and then being a short blonde, always having to prove that there is a brain inside my head. Or maybe it was from watching "Gidget" too many times.

"Go out there and we'll watch you from here and help you," Fred said. "We're going to chill for a while on the beach."

Off I went into the ocean and decided I didn't care if they laughed at me. Although I didn't anticipate getting up that morning, there were so few people on the water that I knew I had to stay in longer and try more. And I did. It wasn't perfect. My timing was off; I fell off or I missed the wave completely, feeling the momentum of the ocean fall still below me.

But as soon as Fred entered the water and called to me how well I was doing, I started to paddle and found myself riding a wave. I didn't stay up long but I was up. I did it! I felt it—how balanced the board was below me that allowed me glide across the water.

He called out, urging me on and then said, "I was going to come out here and push you into the waves but you know what you're doing. I'm going to surf with you if that's okay."

It was okay and it was helpful. He showed me how I was going up too far back on my board and drew a box in the wax, just as Merrick had done in Australia. This made sense. I could feel that, too.

I kept thinking back to junior high when a group of us did gymnastics before school. While I wasn't an athletic kid, in those days I did somersaults and cartwheels on the balance beam, things I never thought I could accomplish. Balancing myself on the surfboard was no different. And I had far surpassed my expectations. While the men I met surfing told me of places with larger waves, I shrugged them off. "I'm not there yet," I said. "But I will be."

No one forced me to do anything I couldn't do, and having Fred call out to me, "Go Michelle!" was much appreciated. I wasn't surfing alone.

But it also was comical when I admitted to him that I started to miss some waves because I was thinking about other things. "You're only supposed to think about surfing while you're out here," he laughed.

I shoved my thoughts of writing away and focused again.

One of their friends came out when I was sitting, waiting for another wave and said, "I can't believe this is only your eighth time surfing. I saw you catch that wave before."

All this time I thought I was doing it wrong. Really I wasn't any different than anyone else.

By the time Scott came out onto the water and showed me more about paddling, turning, and gaining momentum, I'd been out there about an hour and was starting to tire. My arms were getting cold and my focus felt drained. But I did appreciate when he kept calling for me to paddle harder. I could feel that the harder I paddled, the more momentum I gained, and that meant I could catch the wave better.

Scott also reminded me not to look down but to look ahead. This had been the biggest lesson from Sunny in Hawaii, and when I'd done it, focusing on the hotels of Waikiki rather than the board under me, I rode the wave.

It's instinct to look down, to see where the board is, where we are going, rather than to look ahead. Much like life, it's part of being secure, or so we think. If we look down, we won't miss a step or trip on a sidewalk crack. But looking ahead will get us further.

What holds us back in life is much the same as what holds us back in grief. We let our fears dictate where we go, or where we don't go. It would have been easier for me to run my four and a half miles that morning, sit down to write or read the newspaper, and do something else rather than get myself ready to go to the beach. I didn't have to get out of my box. I could have kept my eyes at the top level of the box looking out, thinking about how I didn't really want to venture out into the world but stay where it was comfortable.

I got in the van with my board because I knew I had to. I would be okay even if I surfed alone. I would learn. The ocean tumbled me around a few times that morning, reminding me that I wasn't in charge, just as life reminds me of that when my ego grows too big. The board never hit me in the head or anywhere else, and for that I was grateful. If I hadn't driven down the beach that morning, though, I never would have met any of the locals who were helpful in boosting my confidence in making me a better surfer. I continued to learn, and I was building a community to help me do it. It started with the lessons in all those different places, led me to Jamie and Ethan, and now I had Scott, Fred, and their friends.

It felt good to be included in part of the surfing community. While I could ask Jamie and Ethan questions, it was good to have met people on the beach. I know some people go to the ocean to be alone, and I get that, but having community is important for us as human beings. We all want to feel like we belong, and we have all sorts of communities to belong to in our lives.

Grief isn't any different from life or surfing. If we stay in our box, our room, our bed, or stay stuck, as we often like to say about people, we won't ever see the hope that is still in the world. We let our fears keep us from experiencing what could be our greatest rewards. We forget that hope is stronger than fear.

And the more we get out, the more we talk to people, the more we find people who have been through something like what we have or can offer us helpful perspective. We build a community around us, one that we never thought would be part of our lives because ultimately none of us think about the reality of death and loss until it happens.

But when it does, we find that our friends change because some people can't handle it. It's not bad. I was lucky that many people remained in my life, but I have many more people in my life who are more supportive of me than some of the friends I had before. And I find that the people who gravitate toward me are people who have experienced something similar. While we don't always have to talk about what we've been through, we know that having those shared experiences bonds us in some way.

The more I forced myself to get out onto the ocean, the more I learned. In just a few days, I had propelled myself forward to a place that felt good. I knew I was right where I had to be. While the guys were surprised that I wasn't going to stay on the beach all day (I tried to explain I had a book and newspaper article to write), I knew that hour or so I spent on the water was just enough for me. I would be out there the next day. And by that evening, I would be craving the water again for another conversation. As the water kept teaching me, I was absorbing its lessons as quickly as I could.

9

Christopher Lawford, the son of Patricia Kennedy and actor Peter Lawford, wrote in his book how great his grandmother Rose Kennedy was about being present in the moment. He wrote about how she would take walks with him and she was right there with him. In the time since I read that, I often think about the importance of being in the moment.

So many times people are caught up in the million things they are doing that they don't enjoy the moment they are in. Life is fleeting, as is the gift of time. When we have had a loss, we learn this lesson. Or at least we think we have learned it. Then, after life gets back to the routine, we forget about it until we get slapped with another loss and we are reminded again how precious time is.

I admit that this has been a difficult lesson for me to learn, and sometimes I believe it's why life keeps handing me losses. I was never good at being present. Starting in junior high in particular, I began to daydream about the future. While this did help me cope with difficulties around me as I learned to maneuver everyday life, it also kept me from being as present in my life as I should have. There is a balance to be learned, and I continue to try to master it, but living in the moment is a lifelong challenge for me.

There is another reason that we need to be present in our lives. Only in the present can we receive the messages that help us go forward. Living in the past can often be comfortable, like curling up in a favorite blanket. Thinking about the future is scary. For me, the future was often my comfort. I always found hope in the future because I could always make it up as I wanted it to be. Even in the depths of the loss of my sister and the other events of my life, something has always burned bright in the future for me.

I had to learn to live in the present, though, if I wanted to receive the signs and messages to propel me forward. Running taught me this lesson. If I set out on a three-mile run and all I could think about was finishing, then I never did well. It was as if I jumped too far forward. I had to be present in those three miles, although daydreaming can help them go by quicker.

In surfing, I had to learn to be present all the time. I was learning to watch the ocean, the conditions around me, the surfers near me, people walking on the shore. There was a lot to focus on.

I woke up on Monday morning, my upper body sore from paddling hard the day before. I had felt the momentum underneath me as the board slid across the water. I knew that the harder I paddled, the more momentum I would gain on the wave. Ethan had been right: my paddling was lazy. Merrick had called it my swimming stroke because I was paddling my arms separately rather than together.

Driving to Rat, though, I tried to focus on getting out on the ocean. I'd had a great morning the day before and today would be just as great. When I was on the water, or even driving to the water, I had a sense that I was doing what I was supposed to be doing. Being out there an hour each day felt perfect. I was tired by the time I got back to the house but it was a good tired. It was as if something inside me had been satisfied for at least twenty-hours. I didn't have the need to surf all day but I needed something for a short time and it was being fulfilled.

That morning I had a hard time keeping my mind on the ocean. I was tired, and because I was working with people in the Central and Eastern time zones, they were up and working by the time I rolled into my running shoes, meaning the e-mails were coming in as I left for the beach.

There were few people on the water, making it a perfect morning, and I could finally say that the waves looked good. It was the first time I felt I could look at them and actually make a judgment. Another accomplishment garnered.

I paddled out and watched a few. Today for the first time I didn't feel the need to watch everyone else. Some people were wiping out just as much as me. I knew what I needed to know and it was time that I kept trying. As I lay on the board, I found my mind drifting to working on this book, to the freelance article I was writing, and other things on my agenda. And each time I drifted back to water in front of me, the darkness that made up a coming wave was flying toward me and I was too late to start paddling. Some of them looked good, too.

Then I knew I had to be patient and wait for another one. The ocean is reliable that way. Sometimes we have to wait for a bit but it is about the patience, too. Just like in life we want everything right now and often we believe we should have it now. But it is a process, a journey. And when we reflect back, what we remember most is that process and the journey rather than the event itself.

I heard once that our lives are shaped by the days between as much as by the special days. In that sense, what is considered ordinary time is filled with meaning. We should savor the moments nothing seems to be happening because they are the most special. Our time with our loved ones can't be replaced. We can buy new clothes or replace a toy or most anything else. But we can't get that time back.

Finally, I brought myself back to the water and kept my eyes and my mind on the ocean in front me. I saw a good wave and did my best to whip the board around and start paddling. It didn't feel smooth or fluid but I knew that one day it would—just as the day before I had finally felt somewhat comfortable sitting on the back of my board whereas just twenty-four hours earlier I kept flipping over in the water.

As I paddled forward, I kept thinking of Fred calling to me the day before, "Paddle hard, Michelle!" I wanted to feel my board gliding me across the top of the wave. I started to stand up, still looking down, and promptly fell off. I knew I was looking down because in my mind it's like a repetition of seeing the white and orange of the board below me.

I wasn't deterred. The waves crashed, still keeping me from getting back to the lineup but I let them do their thing and found a break in them where I could paddle back.

I didn't wait that long for the next wave. This one seemed to stop below me. I was learning that when the wave seemed to stopped below me, I simply didn't have the momentum to ride it. I'd watched people ride those same waves before.

But the next wave I attempted to catch was the opposite. I didn't get up soon enough and it came into the back of me, propelling me forward. A few more of these and I was done for the day. I knew it couldn't have possibly been an hour yet but I needed to get my work done. What made it hard to leave was knowing I only had a week and a half more. I was trying to be present and enjoy it as much as I could because I wasn't sure when I would get to do it again. The very notion that we have thrown the energy toward it helps the boomerang of letting it go to bring it back.

10

I long ago learned that not every day in my life would be perfect or great. When we were young my dad used to tease us when we complained about something. "Oh, such problems!" he would say. We hadn't yet learned enough about life to know that the small things we worry about at thirteen aren't so important at twenty, thirty, forty.

My body didn't feel so tired or sore on Tuesday morning as it had on Monday, but my mind was elsewhere. If I didn't know my days on the ocean were limited, I might not have gone at all. I kept thinking about my writing and several other things I had to do later that morning.

After arriving on the beach, I walked down to the second lifeguard station and remembered that Scott had told me the waves break quicker there. I'd done well two days before so I thought it was a good idea to return.

As soon as I slipped my board into the water my problems started. It was breaking so fast that I couldn't get past the break. And when I thought I had made it past, a wave would come up and break quickly, smacking me in the face or almost sending me flying off my board. I didn't feel bad nor did I have a negative attitude; it just wasn't going all that well. When I finally reached a place where I thought I could rest, many good waves kept coming but I found myself not wanting to go. Surfing by myself meant I could sit out there as long as I wanted and no one would know. I knew it wasn't a good thing. It is sort of like not getting out of bed on one of those kinds of days.

I didn't realize how much I got pushed around until I was walking back up the hill and saw my hair, always pulled back in a ponytail, flying everywhere in my shadow, battered from the ocean. With the board under my left arm, I couldn't do anything about it until I got to the top and placed it on the grass in front of the car in the parking lot. When I did feel the back of my head, I realized that my ponytail had been dismantled. The water had gotten the best of me.

While it wasn't a good surfing day, it did feel good to be on the water. When I'm out there, riding the board or paddling around, I have a sense of peace. I am disconnected for a time from my life. The only leash is the leash that keeps my surfboard from floating away from me.

I didn't mind that I carried the board all the way down the hill and back up again without riding a wave. It was okay. Some days are like that.

I kept coming back to the fact that I didn't want to surf alone, though. I didn't want to admit that to anyone, and at the same time I was conflicted. I was afraid of getting in someone's way if I surfed with other people since I didn't have good control of my board yet. It was easier to surf by myself, but it was even easier not to go into the water when I saw the waves since none of the other surfers knew me. No one would make fun of me or ask me later why I didn't go. On Sunday the guys I met didn't ask me when I didn't go into the water, but there was something great about knowing they were on the ocean rooting for me even though they were looking for their own waves to catch.

11

Today, the experience of a sibling who loses a brother or sister to suicide is somewhat different from what I went through. Siblings didn't go to support groups in the years after Denise died, and parents often talked about how their children weren't coping well. Or how they *thought* they weren't coping well. What they didn't understand was that often the surviving siblings wanted their own space to talk about the sibling who died and their experience. Some siblings felt as if their parents weren't interested in them because they were consumed with the child who had died.

When I gave presentations about the unique experience of sibling suicide loss, parents would often come up to me and tell me they had no idea what their children were going through because they were consumed with their own grief. No one does anything maliciously in grief. We might think we know how we will respond when someone dies but we truly don't know until it happens to us. Loss is inevitable for everyone but how we react to it is up to us.

Sibling survivors of suicide have more connections today because there are more support groups and ways to connect via the Internet. In some places, siblings gather without the parents so they can talk about their unique experiences in a place where they won't feel judged by their parents.

I'm happy to know that I helped make this happen for siblings everywhere. Now I know it's my role to show that we can move on from the grief road to a place where the loss doesn't define us.

Talking about the sibling experience was important for me. I needed to understand how the relationship was part of my life and helped define who I am. Before Denise died, I had little understanding of how much time we spend with our siblings, and how that makes up who we are. Denise and I taught each other so much about functioning in life. I hated sharing a room with her but it taught me how to share space with someone else. And it created a whole lot of memories that I wouldn't have if we hadn't had shared a room.

It was important to talk about how the suicide grief experience differs from other types of losses. I didn't need to tell my story so much after a period of time but it was invaluable for people to hear that personal story, so I kept doing it.

People connected to me over my grief experience, coming up to me after talks and wanting to share their own stories. They e-mailed me, and sometimes they called me or sent a letter in the mail. Now they leave notes on Facebook.

What I began to realize though, was that I didn't want to tell the story anymore. I was beginning to feel silly telling people about something that happened almost twenty years ago. People identified me around it but it no longer identified me. I knew it didn't, and I was afraid if I kept telling it, I would never find the doorway out.

12

The more time I spent out on the ocean, the more I began to understand how surfing personifies life and the lessons that I've learned and continued to learn. I could see the importance of the balance and timing. I had to know the exact time to get up on the board, although I struggled with that. Life is much the same. We need to balance all aspects of our lives and understand that the timing isn't all about us. As Ethan said, he would call to Mother Nature, wanting her to send waves, and then realize that he didn't have any control over the ocean. We have little control over much of life except our reactions to what happens to us. It's about faith—faith that we will be okay, faith that we can survive what we've been through.

I have begun to wonder if some of coping with grief is instinctual. It hurt. How can I say that losing my sister didn't hurt? But I see now that the lessons I learned in competitive running prepared me for coping with grief. At first I thought they prepared me for life because mostly it was about inspiring myself, but now I understand it was about the grief journey as well.

In the past eleven years I've basically been teaching people how to grieve. Can we teach others how to grieve? Can we teach people to grieve better? What works for me might not work for someone else. What Merrick taught me in Australia didn't really work for me. He did give me a good lesson in how to keep the surfboard from whacking me in the face, but his stance didn't work well for me. When I returned to surfing in California with Ethan, he reminded me what Merrick taught me and what worked for him.

Each time I talk, I hope that people pull out one thing that works for them. I know in that two-hour lesson with Merrick at Noosa, I learned more than one thing. I just had to tease out what didn't work, although I didn't get that until I surfed the first time in California.

I have never pretended to be something I'm not. It's why I took up surfing. I had wanted to do it for a long time but, as I said before, I was intimidated walking down to the ocean by myself with the board under my arm. I didn't feel I was a bona fide surfer yet but as each day went by and I got in the van each morning to drive to the ocean (after thinking it would be nice just to take a shower and start my day rather than go get beat up in the waves), I felt more accepted. Surfing is part of who I am. I always wanted it to be part of my life, and here I had the chance to make it happen. Life gives us these opportunities, and it's up to us to make them happen.

Surfing also makes me see how the meanings of things have changed in my life. Denise wrote in a journal that our making and eating raw oatmeal cookie dough (essentially sugar, butter, and flour) after my track meets my junior year of high school was what prompted her bulimia. When I read that, I became unable to make oatmeal cookies for a long time. But in my book *Sisters: The Karma Twist* I wrote part of the story around oatmeal cookies. It was my way of changing the sad meaning to something that bonded the two sisters in a happy way.

13

I didn't need to surf with anyone, but I found it more productive when I did. This goes along with the importance of having someone with whom to share our lives. We accomplish more when someone walks the road with us. I thought about Sunday when I was on the water with Fred and Scott, about how they tried to help me and be positive even as I kept tumbling off my board. Life is no different.

To have someone in our lives does help us to be whole because that person can balance out the parts of us that need healing, that need support, and we each have different knowledge to teach the other.

It's been hard for me to accept this. My early experiences taught me that it was better to go alone because I couldn't always rely on someone to be there, whether it was a boy or my sister Denise because she ended her life. I kept my nose stuck in my goals and came out sometimes but found myself disappointed by the men I met so I returned to my goals.

Joe helped me let go of that. We were supportive of each other and we both grew in our time together. However, life circumstances ended the relationship and it was time to move on.

Once the marriage was over, I felt challenged again by what I had felt all those years ago. I was trying hard to be that independent woman. After all, no one wants someone clingy in their lives. We want to enjoy our time with a partner, and we also like the time we have to ourselves. It's a balancing act. But until Ethan began to talk about his girlfriend, I didn't realize how much I struggled with that.

I see now, especially being back on my own, how important it is to who have someone with whom to share the road. Two are stronger than one. But I don't want to be needy in any way. I want a strong love that focuses on that journey ahead of us, the one that has so many unknowns.

Each day I'm driving out to the surf, I keep thinking how I don't want to do it alone, how it would be easier not to go and turn around and just start work for the day. I keep doing it although part of me doesn't feel it's complete unless I'm sharing it. I'm trying to accept that it's okay to feel that way, that it doesn't make me needy or clingy. It's all part of continuing to truly be the person I'm supposed to be.

I also didn't arrive in this place overnight. I still believe it was important for me to be independent all those years ago because it kept me from being in a situation I shouldn't have been in, one that wouldn't have been very happy. However, I did miss out on some love along the way.

14

Lois went to the beach with me one day and I got in the water later than usual. It was a beautiful day, and the shore was crowding up with kids and people walking. I had developed a fear of hitting someone along the shoreline, having come close to a little girl and her mother on my last trip out on the water. You couldn't beat the blue of the water, although I could feel the conditions change as we inched near 10:00 a.m. I had heard from several people that conditions always change around that time in the morning.

Still, I did get a few good tries in. My goal was to focus on looking ahead and not looking down. It still resonated in my ear, Sunny telling me to look ahead at the hotels in Waikiki. When I did that, I sailed across the wave to shore. But here at Rat, I couldn't stop looking down at the white on my board and the black "O.O" in the middle of it. I reminded myself I needed to look ahead at the rocks.

The water was getting choppy and the waves fewer and farther between. I got up on the back of the board a few times but missed the waves. Still I felt confident as the board and I left the water.

I had been posting bits and pieces about my surfing on Facebook. My friend Chris teases me how I'm now a pro surfer since I've been surfing multiple times. There is a view that I'm this great surfer now although the reality is that it will take me a long time to get really good at it. I had to remind myself on Sunday that the men I surfed with had been doing it for thirty years. They grew up surfing, taking it on when they were surely less fearless on the water at twelve and thirteen than they are now at approaching fifty.

Because they did it so young though, it's instinct, like riding a bike. I probably would have been scared to death to surf at a young age. Actually, I would have been more afraid of embarrassing myself and doing something stupid.

That doesn't make me a pro surfer, though. I will never be that. I will probably always be a student of the sport but I will love every minute of it. No matter how little I do on the board, I still love being out there. I watch other people surf or how little they actually surf. I see some twenty-something girls out there catching up about life and probably men. One day I saw a young couple surfing together (and I admit I was envious).

Everyone wants to know if I've gotten up on the board, and I'm sure they assume I'm doing it all the time. At this point I'm not, but I don't care. I'm learning, and each day I see how I can continue to push myself. But I also was never a great athlete. I'm a decent runner because I've been running since I was twelve. I can write because growing up I wrote stories and had friends I wrote to all around the world. I practiced to get where I'm at. And much the same way, I'm practicing each day on the surfboard.

To carry a board under my arm, wearing a wet suit with my hair flying everywhere, feels like a badge of courage. People seem to have more respect for you even if they didn't actually see you surf. They didn't know that I didn't get up, that I was missing the waves. I would have told them the truth, but no one asked.

When Lois and I were leaving, we watched some people roll their boards down the hill on wheels and later she joked to Sam that I was going to get a set of wheels. No way would I do anything but carry the board under my arm. Or maybe on top of my head.

Still, I'm not sure how people think that I might actually surf naked like the bumper sticker my friend Karen gave me in eighth grade. I'm not as daring as people think I am.

The choppiness of the water that day was nothing compared to the next morning. Peering out the window before my run, I could see it was foggy. On top of the hill where Sam and Lois live, it was like we were floating in the clouds. Although you can't actually feel it around you, you could see the wisps of the clouds floating by. Driving down to the ocean two hours later, it still hadn't burned off and I began to wonder if I'd made a mistake. I debated driving back to the house and attempting to go back to the ocean later.

But as I turned onto Hawthorne, the fog disappeared although the clouds remained. The ocean looked rather calm in the cloudiness. It wasn't the crystal blue of the day before, but it didn't matter. I pulled on my wet suit and waded into the water. There were as many surfers as the day before.

As I made my way past the breaks, it occurred to me that I only had a week left in California. How much progress had I made in my surfing? Surely, I should be further along, I told myself. That meant I had to take more chances. I had to get over my lazy paddling and do it hard and remember how it felt when that momentum underneath propelled me forward.

I set to it but found the conditions of the ocean vastly different in the cloudiness. For the seasoned surfers, this wasn't a big deal. They were used to picking them. I felt a little lost without the sun to darken the water where the waves were starting and to sprinkle light on the breaks you can see on top of the waves.

I couldn't blame the ocean. Yes, it was harder to read the waves, but life isn't the same every day. Grief isn't even the same each day. Some days we feel better than others. Clouds make some of us feel sad and energize others. I wasn't going to be a fair-weather surfer. I'd never been a fair-weather runner. If something is important to us, we go out and do it each day.

Yet so many times we do blame the conditions and others for what we're feeling or if something doesn't go right. I'm guilty of that. Two weeks before leaving for Los Angeles, I had a morning where everything seemed to be slightly off. My iPod Shuffle wasn't working right, and then I tripped twice on my run. I could easily have let that dictate my day, but I told myself I wasn't going to. And I didn't. Just because it was cloudy and I couldn't see the waves as well as usual, I wasn't going to let this be a bad surfing experience.

We can't blame the environment because we don't control it. And if we think we can control the ocean, just as Ethan thought he could when he was younger, the ocean will throw something at us to remind us that it's stronger than we are. It's about changing our reactions to life events and the environment. And when we do that, we find that life is easier.

The ocean felt calm in the clouds, not like an angry storm. I didn't get much done, but I worked on paddling harder and my arms felt a little sore as I walked back up the hill with my board under my arm.

15

It was cloudy again, although not the foggy weirdness that had enveloped us in Palos Verdes the day before. I felt tired as I drove back to the ocean. Sam had joked with Lois the day before that he couldn't leave the couch all afternoon because he was experiencing SAD, Seasonal Affective Disorder, since the sun hadn't been out all day. I was beginning to think it was bothering me as well. Living in New Mexico, I thrived on the sunshine and dry air. I didn't feel weighted down in humidity or clouds that hovered too low. I'd been lucky that despite the heat in southern Los Angeles, the days I'd been there were filled with sun.

It would be another wet suit day. Part of me wanted to drive to the ocean and drive straight back. Another part of me didn't mind walking all the way to the beach with my board and then turning back without going in the water. I couldn't do that, though. I had only six more days of surfing. Somehow I had to get out there, even though I kept thinking maybe a day off was in order.

My arms were tired. I felt like I needed someone to push me. I'd always been the one to motivate myself, so much so that few people tried to motivate me. I came off as overly motivated, so I often was left alone to do my thing. In the past year, though, I'd realized how much I needed someone to push me and help me to be better. It often feels like I'm inspiring others, which I'm happy to do, but who is inspiring me?

I had started talking to myself the day before, probably because there was no one around me on the ocean. Few surfers were out today, and I could sense the sun would be back later; it wouldn't be as dark as the previous day.

"I have to get up today," I told myself. Even before I entered the ocean, I stood on the shore, my leashed Velcroed and my board under my arm and said out loud, "Help me get up today. I have to get up."

It didn't go very well. The waves looked okay. I was by myself. I missed a few completely although I could see them coming better. And one time my mind wandered while I was turned sideways and a larger wave broke right under me, sending the board, and me, flying.

I wasn't deterred, but I felt too tired to focus. It still wasn't like riding a bicycle.

Getting out of the water, I thought about the ways my vocabulary had changed over the past week. I truly had had no idea what it meant for a wave to break. The meaning of the word felt different in surfing. Maybe I'd heard these terms over time but they meant little until I was out there on the board waiting for one. "Catching a wave" meant more than before I'd actually done it. I thought of surfing as riding a wave but it never occurred to me that I was actually catching it, especially after I let some of them get away from me.

While I felt a little sad, not knowing how much surfing I'd get in until spring, I saw how much life had changed for me in a short time. I owned a wet suit and a surfboard. I felt like I had a new activity I could list on Facebook and anywhere else I'm asked what I do. I surf. I finally felt like I'd earned the term Surfer Girl.

Watching other people surf, I found myself rooting for them, especially the kids and the girls who were younger than me (which was probably all of them). While I was envious watching them carrying their boards on their heads going down to the beach, I smiled at them and knew they were lucky to live in a time where girls' surfing is accepted.

I was never told there wasn't anything I couldn't do but I also never asked if I could surf. I covered sports in high school for the student newspaper and then ventured into it, not on purpose, in college. I was considered an anomaly then, doing a job in a man's world. They brought the athletes to me in the hallway rather than taking me into the locker room. I didn't care; I had a job to do.

Title IX, creating equal opportunities in sports for women, was enacted a year after I was born. It turned forty just months after I did. The reality is that girls in the twenty-first century have more opportunities than I did in the late 1980s, but we didn't think things were bad. When it appeared that I was on the road to a career in sports journalism, no one deterred me. Maybe my road paved the way for other girls.

If I have a daughter, she will be on that surfboard. She will go to surf camp and be out there with the other kids I pass by each day on the beach. Surfing will build her resilience and confidence in ways I never could have imagined in my own youth. I still see the possibilities as endless in my life but hers will be even bigger than mine.

16

I used to love to watch the television show *Gidget.* I was too young for the original, with Sally Field, instead watching the later one with Gidget and her husband, Moondoggie, in their twenties and coping with married life. The show was on in syndication around dinnertime during the weekend.

My only recollection of the show is the episode where they buy their dream house and then realize how hard they have to work to keep it, taking time away from each other, and in the end decide to return to their old house. It wasn't until later that I learned that the television show and movie were based on the book *Gidget, the Little Girl with Big Ideas,* written by Frederick Kohner and published in 1957. The real Gidget, Kathy Kohner, wanted to learn to surf and told her father about the people she met on the beaches of Malibu. Her father turned those stories into the book, making Gidget world famous.

While I was in Los Angeles, Terry Tracy died. Tracy was the model for the *Gidget* character the Big Kahuna, and his obituary states that he quit surfing in 1980 because he said people who are over the age of forty and surf look stupid. Clearly, he didn't go to Rat Beach in 2012 where the median age of surfers looked to be forty (my age). The sport has come a long way from the 1950s but the people who were young then are still surfing now. It's something any of us can do as long as we're near a body of water that has waves big enough and our bodies hold up.

Still I wondered, Was he right? Did I look stupid now that I was forty and surfing? I quickly dismissed the thought, especially when I got to the beach on Saturday morning and saw the wide range of ages of people who were surfing. (Of course, I always have to remind myself that I don't look forty!)

I began to wonder if my body knew I was forty. I felt a strange sensation on my knee for the third day in a row on the walk down to the beach from the parking lot. I carry my board under my left arm on the walk down and, thinking it was a balance issue, I tried to walk with it under my right arm on the way back up. I am left-handed, though, so it was much easier to use the strength of my left side. I gave up the notion of balance.

It was cloudy again and most people were wearing their long wet suits. I didn't want to get in, thinking it felt cold just standing there on the shore. But the waves are good at crashing me just right, getting me wet, and showing me that it's not as cold as I think it is. Once I'm in, I forget how cold it is and think only about finding a wave to catch and getting up on it. The water didn't look rough, but when I got out onto it, I could feel it was somewhat choppy, my board bouncing against it.

I had to get it. I paddled around, still working at making my paddling less lazy. My arms felt a little sore each time I paddled but that meant I was doing something right. There were few surfers, and I watched some people wipe out while others rode those small waves, gliding close to the sand beneath them.

I wanted to blame the waves because they were small. But I knew it wasn't the waves; it was me. I was missing them, getting on them too late. I saw them coming, my turns getting quicker, my paddling getting better, but I was getting up too late, and when my feet were below me on the board, the wave had passed and there was nothing to take me forward.

I kept mumbling to myself, looking for a good wave and trying to get up quicker. I wished I had someone to tell me when to get up, but I knew what to do. It was a matter of me getting it right. And I know that when I get it right, there will be no stopping me.

After a while, I'd had enough and told myself I'd try to catch one more wave and let it lead me back to shore.

I paddled hard, I got on top of it, I felt it right under me. But before I could let my hands go, it was gone. Still, I finally had the timing right. Always at the end I seem to get it right.

When I stood on the beach taking my leash off, I felt the wind and didn't second-guess leaving. Tomorrow would be better, I thought, also hoping the sun might be back in the morning.

17

"Tough feet, eh?" a voice said behind me as I crossed the pavement to the sand at the bottom of the hill on Sunday morning.

I had been aware of someone coming up behind me, but people usually kept going and didn't speak as they went by. I looked up to see a man next to me wearing a black shirt and black shorts with a yellow towel thrown around his neck. And a baseball hat. My first thought was that he reminded me of Lance Armstrong. It was the yellow. But it wasn't a good time to be reminding anyone of Lance since it was just a few days after he'd been stripped of his Tour De France titles.

I had to laugh at what he said to me though. I'd grown up running barefoot around the neighborhood, and almost never wore shoes at home, often complaining at conferences that my feet didn't feel right. It was only when I remembered that I wasn't used to wearing shoes that I realized why my feet didn't feel right.

But walking outside, my feet aren't so happy barefoot anymore. Still, I didn't want to carry any shoes down to the beach with me. Although it had been difficult to leave behind all the "stuff" in the van the first few days of surfing, I'd gotten used to it. Several people had told me there was nothing to worry about but I thought it was better not to worry at all.

I'd also gotten used to walking down the hill, first on pavement and then the sand, in my bare feet, although that also meant I was walking slower between getting used to the rocks underneath me and carrying the board on my side.

My feet were getting tougher but it also meant I couldn't walk as fast as I was used to. The competitive runner in me hates to be passed by anyone, walking, running, baby jogger, anything.

The man in the baseball hat suggested a pair of shoes like his and then began to tell me how he'd been living there for some years but yesterday was his fiftieth birthday and he was committing himself to spending time on the ocean he hadn't taken advantage of in all the years of living there.

"I tried that," he said, pointing at my board. "It was hard."

"I didn't say I was very good but I still like it," I responded.

He said paddleboarding was next on his list.

We parted ways at the large rocks right before the beach sand starts and I walked down the shore seeing there were not even a handful of surfers in the water. The early morning had been cloudy. The sun was out, but the air was still cool. I'd gone without the wet suit, and told myself the sun would keep me warm.

More people were talking to me, and cars were looking familiar in the parking lot. My visit to PV was coming to an end, and I wasn't sure when I'd be back. Still, it was nice to be acknowledged. It also gave me a sense of safety. If something happened to me, people might help me. While I've only been hit by the board once, back in New Hampshire, I never forget that the ocean can be unpredictable.

Standing ankle-deep in the water, I noticed the waves were small, almost nonexistent. That explained why the water was empty of surfers.

Still, I should have been able to ride them even though it meant just skimming the surface. To my right, a dad was teaching his son how to surf. They weren't good waves, though. I didn't see crackling at the top of any of them. I tried a few and missed. I lay out there so long I felt like I was sunbathing on the board except that I couldn't look down because the water movement under the board made me dizzy. It wasn't restful but it was good. The sun was warm, filling me with strength.

I paddled south, to my left, and encountered another couple surfing. "Pretty small today, huh?" he asked.

"Yes," I agreed and adding, "I want to bag it but the sun feels good."

The waves were better there. A bit bigger and some crackling at the top.

I tried to go and while I sat on top of the wave, I realized my arms were too sore to sustain holding up my body until I popped up. I didn't think they were sore and wondered how that had happened. I hadn't worked that hard yesterday paddling, or had I? Trying not to paddle lazily was taking its toll.

I despondently paddled back to the lineup and wondered if I could get up. I thought about getting out, but I knew I had the time. It was Sunday, and the water was still fairly empty.

So I tried again. Sitting right on top of the wave, in the exact place I should have been, the same thing happened. My body wasn't going to get me up today. It was time to go.

When I reached the top of the hill, a group of runners were standing around talking. I wasn't sure if they were waiting to start or had finished their run but one of the women asked me if the water was cold.

"Yes," I said, looking for the right way to say that even though it felt cold when I got in, I forgot about it after getting wet. I always hate when I first get wet. The waves always take care of that in the ocean though. "Yeah yeah yeah," I'd say after getting crashed on. "I get your hint," and I'd hop on the board and paddle toward the lineup.

"It's cold, but the sun's out and all is well," I finally said, rounding the turn and walking away from them toward the van.

"You're right," she said. "It is a beautiful day."

I placed the board on the grassy area to open the car and towel off before driving back to the house. My feet were always sandy and I never seemed able to scrape all the sand off, trailing it through Sam and Lois's house and leaving most of it in the bathtub during my shower.

I tried to wipe my feet on the thick grass but it wasn't working. Something made me feel alive doing that, though. I had been in the water feeling the sand below my feet, the water carrying me across the waves. Now I was basking in the sun, drying off. I felt like a solar panel absorbing as much energy as I could. All I could think of was no matter how bad things might be going, there was strength in connecting to the earth. If we take the time to be outside and part of nature, how can we feel bad? I could see how all my years of running had paid off way past the physical benefits.

Yes, surfing is life but it does make me appreciate the details.

18

I had just three days left to surf before departing California. I was going to miss going to the ocean each morning but I knew I'd be back—I just didn't know when. What I did feel good about was how far I'd come.

For so long, particularly as a competitive runner, I berated myself when I didn't do well enough. It wasn't enough to finish a race or to do better than most of my fellow runners. No outcome ever made me happy. It was a tough lesson to learn to be happy with how I did, to relish the small victories. We can't move forward all the time. We don't function at 100 percent every day or in everything we do.

While there were people who continued to believe that I could surf waves bigger than me, I knew better, and I was okay with that. The ways in which I'd improved and what I'd learned were endless. It was hard to believe it was just a year since I first stepped on a surfboard and rode my first wave after just a few tries.

And here I was just about month after a visit to Palos Verdes where, when I mentioned surfing, Lois and Sam said, "Oh sure, we can make that happen."

Putting on that bikini we'd pieced together—$5.00 bottoms on clearance at TJ Maxx and the $17.00 top at Target—meant more now than it did a few weeks ago when I bought it. Getting a surfboard and going out on the ocean by myself felt so foreign and seemed very difficult. I didn't think it was as easy as it felt now. But I also wouldn't have known that if I hadn't tried and given myself the opportunity reach past all the reasons I thought would hold me back.

It's easy to let life hold us back, particularly when we believe we might not be good at something or when it's more comfortable not to do it. But if I had done that, I'd never be where I am now in my life or with my grief experience.

I had done well in speech class in high school and, while I got a little nervous before speaking, it was never something that would incapacitate me as the way running did. Speaking in front of a thousand people is a piece of cake compared to pushing myself to run past any previous limits I had exceeded. For years it had been important to me to beat my own best running successes, but it wasn't now. Instead, I used what I had learned for speaking.

A certain amount of tension is important before competition or before speaking. That level of intensity helps us make sure we are ready to do something. Many times people ask me if I'm nervous, and there are very few times I feel the way I did ten years ago. I've gotten accustomed to being in front of large groups with the focus on me. That comfort has allowed me to expand what I talk about and how I interact with the audience. No more is it just about how I give the talk I've prepared but also how I look out at the faces, how what I say engages them, and now how flexible I can be if something unexpected happens along the way.

Speaking at the Compassionate Friends Conference had been one of those experiences. It was the first time that I would address that group and it was important for me because it wasn't a group devoted to suicide but one that would expand my reach to the more generally bereaved. For them, it was important because I was a suicide survivor and I was a sibling. The organization is for parents and children who have lost a loved one to any type of death, yet siblings and suicide survivors don't often get the opportunity to speak to the entire group of attendees.

Several people at my table asked me if I was nervous. I think I might have disappointed them when I confessed that I wasn't. The tension was there, but I felt more relaxed than usual. I had been asked to speak about my experience as a sibling survivor of suicide. What they didn't know was that I couldn't delve into that experience as I once had. I had no interest in discussing that road anymore. I had begun to tell people to read my first book if they wanted to know more about it, yet I also explained that I wasn't sure I would write that same book anymore because of all that I had learned about myself and the grief experience since it had been published. It continued to sell well, and I knew people, mostly siblings, related to it, but I had moved on.

Instead, I focused on what I had learned and where I was going from here, what this book is based on. Without the last few talks I gave, discussing my new journey, I'm not sure I would have come up with the idea to write this book.

But I also talked about surfing. When I ran into Pat Loder, the Executive Director of Compassionate Friends, in the elevator just hours before I was to speak, and about an hour after I checked in, she was relieved to see me. "I kept asking my staff if you'd checked in yet," she said, breathing a huge sigh.

"Oh. I was surfing," I told her.

I couldn't attend the conference. I didn't want to focus my energy on going to sessions I was no longer interested in. I needed to do things for me although when I arrived in Los Angeles a few days before, I had no idea that surfing would be among them. Nor did I know how much I would change in those few days, buying the surfboard just a few short weeks later.

And so I talked about what surfing was teaching me. It felt like a lot, even though there was much more ahead of me that I wasn't aware of. What amazed me most was that after my talk, after the banquet had ended and a line formed to talk to me, making me one of the last people out of the ballroom, about half of the people in line wanted to discuss surfing with me.

And in the days and weeks ahead, people friended me on various social media sites and said they hoped I'd enjoyed my surfing in Southern California.

I didn't need to talk about my grief experience. It was slowly inching its way out of my talks. That's how I wanted it to be.

19

Jamie the surf shop owner saved my second-to-last day of surfing.

I had read online that the surf at Rat would be around four feet at 7:53 a.m. I had been getting there at 8:30 and thought I could get there earlier, but when I pulled into the parking lot, no one was there.

A woman carrying a paddleboard called out to me to have fun. I wanted to ask, "Does anyone here ever say anything else?" But instead I asked her if she had fun. "Of course," she said. "It's like Hawaii!" While the days were much warmer than the usual California weather, I wasn't complaining about the water being warmer than usual.

I walked down to the beach. The water was clear of surfers except for one. I could see a few further north, but it looked like everyone else was paddleboarding. The waves were better than yesterday. I could see the crackling again, glistening in the sun.

I hadn't been out very long when the other man surfing came up to me and complained that it was too hot. He wore a baseball cap, and his overweight body seemed to be held together by his wet suit. "I hadn't been out on the water in a few weeks and I was starting to feel fat," he said. Had he been reading my mind?

I didn't think not surfing was enough to give him that many rolls under the wet suit. He was nice, I have to say that. However, he began to talk about immigration, which then turned into telling me my board was too short for a beginner. And then he decided I needed a surfing lesson. By now I was hoping I would never sit next to him at a dinner party. He told me everything I was doing wrong, which was, well, everything. "You don't have to surf out here in exile," he said, pointing toward the surfers at the north end. "There's a group of us that meet over there."

I was glad when he finally paddled off. After a few minutes, another surfer appeared, a young Asian man. He smiled at me and said, "Hi."

I bodysurfed back to the shore. I had had enough for the day.

But that afternoon I stopped by Jamie's shop to pick up a cover for the board. The reason most boards look yellow is because of sun exposure, and I wasn't going to let my pristine board go yellow.

We talked for a while when a man, named Brian I would later learn, came in and started talking boards with Jamie. Brian asked about my surfing, and Jamie said something I truly appreciated.

"She's really dedicated." That is the single line that has defined my life and who I am. From writing to running to finishing degrees, I never gave up. When I showed up for cross-country practice my freshman year of high school, I was consistently last on the team. I was No. 21, but I kept at it and made varsity, No. 7, by the regional meet. I knew how hard work paid off, and I knew it would be the same in surfing. The more I do it, the better I will get, even if I don't get to surf every day.

In the same way, I never gave up in my grief. I kept going forward even when I had to stop and walk all those times in the first year after Denise died. And now I was going to keep going with my surfing. I was still learning, but I'd come such a long way.

I know it didn't seem that way to everyone else. All they cared about was whether or not I got up on the board. I knew it was more than that. I could read the ocean better, and the next day I would learn that I was just a few paddle strokes away from riding a wave.

20

It was my last day in Los Angeles. The skies were a perfect blue, and my hours were numbered. Labor Day weekend was just a few days away, and I was due back home. Jamie had said he might make it out to surf that morning, and I looked for him when I got down to the beach but once again saw only a few people. The surf was rising, and I was going to miss a good weekend.

"I'll be back," I said when people asked me to stay longer.

I did see what looked like a familiar figure and board—Scott. I wasn't sure it was him so I walked straight into the water and looked for the few-and-far-between waves. Finally he paddled out and we waited for the waves together. Scott continued to give me tips: helping me with my turns, explaining where in the wave I needed to be, and finally offering positive support when I tried to get up. And didn't.

"You're about three strokes too short on the paddle," he said after I once again fell off the board. Finally, an explanation for the error I kept making. I was too early in the wave, and that was knocking me off.

Then I almost caught it. I had it. I was up. I didn't stay up, though, and fell off again. "You just about had that one," he called to me. I shook my head.

"Don't be scared of it," he said, me lying on my board and him sitting on his.

"I'm not scared!" I retorted.

"You're right," he said, catching himself. "I saw you come through the middle of that wave the other day. You're not scared."

Although the waves were better, there still weren't enough for us to catch, and we both began to feel tired from being on the water. As I dragged my board from the water and under my arm to the guard stand where I could lean it, I didn't feel as sad as I had thought I might. Somehow, something told me, I would be back. I had to let it go and instead focused on talking with Scott and Brian, who had shown up hoping to see Jamie and me surfing.

"Gidget!" he called, making Scott laugh.

I didn't have to hurry back to the Blooms' house but I knew that I wasn't wearing enough sunscreen and I was feeling the heat on the back of my legs. I didn't want to return to Chicago a lobster.

As I carried the board up the paved road one last time, I knew I had come a long way. I was different. I had no idea what a difference a surfboard would make in my life. No matter what had happened on the board, it was like I had told a man a few days earlier. "It's better to be out here than not at all."

21

From seventh grade on, I had a life I dreamed of. While I no longer anticipate that I will marry Simon Le Bon or Bryan Adams (nor do I want to now), I still have my dreams. Even though we fought as most siblings do, Denise still knew more about me than anyone else in my life. It was only in speaking that I came to realize she had been my biggest cheerleader all those years and that even in death, she still is my biggest cheerleader.

Denise was the sister who got me the Eddie Bauer application so I could get a job there during my Christmas breaks during college. And now she is the sister who is still walking the road with me, helping me to publish my fiction, find that fairy-tale ending in my love life, and live out my other dreams like riding waves around the world on a surfboard. I heard someone say that his deceased grandfather moves the chess pieces of his life. I believe that happens to all of us to some extent after our loved ones have died. They are with us, they want us to be happy, and there is much comfort in knowing that they are helping us to achieve the happiness we hope for.

A friend told me that my divorce would be a time to reinvent myself. I could see this to some extent before I became aware of all the changes in my life where the two roads that made up my life were converging again. But what I found after I moved was that I wasn't reinventing myself so much as I was returning to who I truly was at my core. I see that I am the Michelle I always was.

This doesn't mean I didn't like myself all those years or that I regret any road that I traveled. It was what it was supposed to be. I was married and learned a lot from that marriage, and I still appreciate what Joe brought to my life. There are many reasons I am grateful to him. But it was time for us to move forward into other relationships if we were truly to be who we were supposed to be. It doesn't matter what anyone else thinks or believes. We thought we would be together for the rest of our lives, but it didn't work out. And now we go forward on other roads.

I did everything I was supposed to do in the suicide and grief field. Some people worried when I walked away that it would look as if I wasn't happy about what I have accomplished. It is just the opposite; I have learned so much about myself and I believe I have contributed much more than I ever thought I might have, or than I might have with that appearance on *The Oprah Winfrey* show that never happened (yet!). I am very grateful for all the chances I had to speak, to meet new people, to be in the media. I seized each one of these opportunities and learned from all of them.

Without those experiences, I wouldn't be who I'm supposed to be. I wouldn't be ready to launch myself into a larger audience if I hadn't honed my skills in suicide and loss. I am who I am because of what I've experienced, and now I'm ready to move forward to a larger playing field where I will have the opportunity to inspire more people. I have an opportunity right now to carve out the life I always dreamed of.

A high school friend from track came to visit me in our hometown for his twentieth reunion several years ago. He hadn't been back in some time and wanted to eat at Dunkin' Donuts because he was living in a western state where there is no Dunkin'. As we sat there eating the donuts that we enjoyed years ago, I began to talk about a classmate of mine whose books had reached the *New York Times* bestseller list.

She and I had been high school rivals in many ways, our journeys running parallel. As seniors we had shared the title Journalist of the Year for our service on the newspaper staff. When I looked at a timeline on her web site, I saw that we had been seeking publishers for our fiction at the same time in the late 1990s. The difference was that she got signed to a major publisher and her chick lit career took off. I signed with a small publisher who was willing to take a chance on my work and led me to a different road.

People were constantly reminding me that she had made the bestseller list, although no one was malicious about it. Although there was a time when I hoped my work on suicide grief would make it to the bestseller list, I finally realized this would never happen and I would have to write about something else if it was that important to reach that goal. Still, I struggled with what this meant, wondering why she had gotten there and I hadn't.

After telling Bart this, he swallowed his donut and said, "Maybe she's gone as far as she can. Maybe she's achieved all that she is supposed to and you are still climbing."

I don't know where her career is headed, and it ultimately doesn't matter. But what I do know is that I am still climbing. I can see how much my life has changed and propelled me forward in the few years since that conversation. It's almost like when I'm paddling hard and feel the momentum of the wave underneath my board sending me forward. I might not be standing on it yet, but it's there and it's happening. I also might not understand why it is the way it is but just because I don't get on the wave at the right time doesn't mean that I'm not going forward. Maybe it's not the right wave at that time, but the right one will come along. I know that I can rely on the ocean for that.

22

The summer of 1993, when I was at the Olympic Training Center in Colorado Springs, I had a conversation with one of the athletic trainers who came in for two weeks to work at the center. They stayed in the spare room at the end of the hallway of our dorm. We were discussing the grief I was enduring because of my sister's death. He said to me, "You will always be the same Michelle. You will like the same things and do the same things."

At the time I didn't believe him. I wrote about this in my first book. How could that be true? Life had completely changed. I couldn't possibly be the same person ever again. And when I spoke, I told this story repeatedly. But when I started to feel the change in myself, I realized I was that person. I was the same Michelle at my core, and the more I allowed her to come through, the more I could sense that I was she. It felt good to have returned to who I was all those years ago. Of course I'd like to think I'm a more mature version of that Michelle, but I am still she. I am surfing, I have returned to my fiction, I'm carving out the life that I always dreamed of. I'm not completely sure how I will make it happen, but I know I'm on the right road. When I'm on the board, I feel that it's where I'm supposed to be. Life might not keep me in Los Angeles, but there are many places where I can take my board and surf. I have already proven that I can surf in multiple places so why stop now?

If I hadn't traveled to all the places and spaces that life took me to over the past twenty years, I might not have ever made it back to this place. I am lucky, but I have worked hard to get here and it's my reward.

23

I often joke that we all bring assorted luggage with us on life's journey. None of us have the same-sized pieces, and some of us have luggage that is pink or plaid. What we bring to a relationship depends on that unique baggage, our personal experience. And when two people are trying to grieve the same loss, that creates challenges because of their unique backgrounds. Losing a loved one at a young age brings unique struggles—another piece of luggage that we didn't plan to carry. Yet few people address the topic of intimate relationships and how loss impacts them.

For all the ways that life has propelled me forward since the loss of my sister, this is the one area that has been and still to some extent remains difficult for me. In the first years after Denise's death, I struggled to keep a relationship going. I found myself wanting to end it but not understanding why until a friend pointed out that I had to end it in order to control it. My sister had chosen to end her life. I had no control over her decision to do that and the aftermath of that decision.

I find myself repeating this pattern, and I now have to work through it to change it. Denise's death, while she didn't mean it to, left me with a sense of abandonment and rejection that I have to work extra hard to overcome. The hardest part is that we aren't always conscious of what we're doing; we can sabotage something without realizing it.

If there was one thing I knew my sister wanted for my life, it was for me to be happy. I wasn't always the nicest sister to her, mostly because we were often relegated to play together, which also meant that people associated us as one— Michelle and Denise. I wanted to be Michelle. It's no one's fault (this means you, Mom!) because we're all unique people and we never know what will affect us as we get older.

As I traveled through my life, it remained important for me to be independent Inevitably there were hurts in my life, and I had begun to think it was easier to travel through life independently. After all, it's easier to accomplish our goals than it is to sit tight in a relationship, especially when the other person is not behaving the way we had hoped. However, life is meant to be shared. It took me time to understand that.

Sure, I wanted a relationship, but I saw that I needed to be Michelle, not associated with anyone else. It was on my trip to Los Angeles, through the conversation with Ethan, that I began to understand that I could be independent but still part of a couple. It also was because time was beginning to teach me that life truly was about love.

For the first time, I began to see how important it is that we do spend our lives as part of a couple, but that doesn't mean that we let go of any part of ourselves. While in my marriage to Joe I knew that two were stronger than one and we could accomplish more as a couple, it wasn't until I was back on my own that I saw how I needed to learn to balance this again. I began to understand that I wasn't twenty-two anymore. I am forty. I am ready to spend my life with someone and maybe have that family experience.

As I have always said, Denise knew more about me than anyone else. She knew about the goals and the dreams I've had my whole life. If she were here, she might even remember some that I have long buried. She also knew about the boys I had crushes on, and she was sad herself when one particular relationship of mine didn't work out. It left her disappointed in men and by their behavior.

One of her last Christmases though, when she gave me those two glasses, with the words "for when you have someone in your life," not *if*, truly speak to what she wanted for me. While my experiences continued to make me believe that I needed to be independent and do everything without anyone else (including a higher power), she still believed that there would be someone for me.

While I long ago let go of the fact that I never told her that I loved her in life, I know that she knows that from where she is now. She's still with me. She's still cheering for me. And she knows that I will still have my fairy-tale ending, even on days when it's hard for me to believe it.

While I move forward onto my converged roads, I also know there are places I am not fully healed. I'm not sure that any of us are fully healed in any place in life. If we were, there would be no reason for us to go on.

I'm aware that some of these places for me may involve someone else joining me for that healing to come. I don't know how or when that will happen. Ethan said about his girlfriend that she could not be the love he had for his grandmother. But his girlfriend can be there with him and be the love that he needs, a love that I believe his grandmother brought to him.

For me, I know this part of my journey is just beginning to play out.

Part VI

1

No matter how our loved ones died, they wouldn't want us to live in grief the rest of our lives. They want us to live happy lives, to laugh and love and enjoy what can still be ours. We don't have to cling to the sadness that they aren't with us. We have the memories, and no one can take those away from us.

Denise didn't love herself, and at that time of her life, her pain felt insurmountable. That doesn't diminish her love for any of us. When life hands me cracked raw eggs, I have to remind myself of that hope she had for me. She might not have had it for herself, but even in her pain, and now as she cheers me on from where she's at, she had it for me.

We also have choices about our futures. Grief is an opportunity to live life more fully. I can't take the past back; I can't go back and redo anything that has happened. But what I can do is make the most of the road ahead of me.

I don't know what that road holds for me right now. None of us do; we can't and we shouldn't. While I like to know what's coming around the corner, I have learned that I can't see the future. Life is about how we react to situations and use them to help us grow and be in the moment.

It's just like when I'm lying on that board in the water, waiting for the next big wave worth trying to catch. I don't know when it's going to come nor do I know how long I'll be waiting. But I'm present in that moment enjoying the sun warming my body and feeling the movement of the water below me.

As Sam and I put my board safely into the Blooms' garage before we left for the airport so I could fly back to Chicago, I was sad to cover it up and leave it there. But I also knew that this was just the beginning of my surfing life. My conversations with the water aren't over. As I continue to travel through life, they will continue to be part of my journey.

2

We do not have to be defined by the losses that make up our life story. Yes, they are part of us. Some people have been afraid that if I move forward, I will deny all that I have been through and learned. That's far from true. Each experience, although there are many I would rather not remember, is part of what weaves the fabric that comprises the quilt squares of my life. Some experiences I have yet to talk about. Those are coming in the next few books. Grief is woven into them somehow as well. I know that, and I know that this book doesn't mean I will ever stop talking about my sister and the effect of her death on my life. My focus won't be on her in the future, but rather on me and where I'm going. The key is not letting the past dictate our future.

I believe that any of us can overcome anything that happens to us. We experience loss, or what we perceive as loss, all the time. Grief teaches us about ourselves, but it also teaches us about our relationship with the person that we have lost. My relationship with Denise wasn't perfect, and I'm always clear about that when I speak. I am the sister who put the tape on the floor, the one who thought I was being nice by taping her way out of the bedroom that we shared. I tried so hard to separate myself from her, mainly because I was trying to be independent. I didn't understand that independence can be detrimental at times. But I was young. I had to experience life to truly understand and change.

I have learned that we need to be present in the moment because we don't know what will happen outside that moment. We have to take the time to acknowledge what we feel. Once in a support group, a woman named Joan with whom I worked stopped me from handing someone a tissue. She explained later that's it's important to let those tears fall and that person be in the depths of what he or she is feeling. I always thought by offering tissues we are letting people know we care but I realize now that we also need to let them feel where they are at before they can move forward.

Life is filled with big and little moments, big and little lessons. When I slipped off my surfboard one morning in California, I understood why I had to wax it. Quite honestly, I had no clue before. It was a small experience and a small lesson, but one that I only understood by experience. I can't say I like all the lessons I've learned and continued to learn, but I do know that when I look back, I understand. I tell people that when we are in the thick of it, especially when the pain pierces us and we wonder if getting out of bed is worth it, we don't get it. We have to somehow keep working.

In much the same way, surfing forces us to be present. Otherwise we miss the waves. We must get wet; we must feel the cold water. It's all about being in the moment and letting life wash over us. It's also about forgetting our worries, fears, or anything else while we are on the water because we have to keep our eyes peeled, looking for the crackles in the water breaks. Although I like to say that I'm a person who doesn't miss opportunities, for the number of waves I've missed, I wonder how many life opportunities I've missed as well. But then more always come along.

I didn't know when I started writing this book that this is how it would turn out. When I began, I didn't own a surfboard and didn't know I would buy one either—a custom one no less. I didn't know how much surfing epitomized life, especially mine. Maybe that was why surfing attracted me so many years ago, but I wasn't ready to get on the water because I needed to experience life first. All the people I met who started surfing young learned to catch waves and then experienced life, but I had to experience life before surfing.

What surprised me most was how little fear I had on the ocean. I didn't mind getting battered by the waves. I wanted to get right back out there and try it again, and keep trying it until I got it. I didn't care about being underwater, or that sometimes hours later, ocean water would drip out of my nose unexpectedly. I know that life often throws us around, much like the waves pull us away from the direction we want to go. Have I gotten used to it? I know my perspective on what bothers me has changed. My tolerance is much higher for so many things. I still struggle and continue to learn lessons in various parts of my life, but I have moved forward.

Part of moving forward is forgiving—life, people, situations, whatever. There is forgiveness in hope. It's about letting go of what doesn't work, of what holds us back. I can't say that I ever said that I forgave my sister for ending her life because I was never that mad at her about it. Maybe it was because to some extent I realized that the pain she was in far outweighed her hope, especially at seventeen. I couldn't be mad at her when she couldn't see beyond two feet in front of her to feel the love we had for her.

3

Pamela Joye knew little about this book when I talked to her about taking a photograph for the cover. The initial idea had been a photo of me standing with my back to the camera with my board in hand, looking toward the ocean. We were planning to go to a beach in Maine to take the photo. When Pamela suggested Rye, New Hampshire, though, I realized I was going right back to where I had learned to surf, almost exactly a year later.

When I arrived in Boston, waiting at Logan Airport for my friend Mary Ann to pick me up, I could smell the sea air (and garlic bread). Even though I still didn't live near it and I'm not sure I ever will, the ocean had become home for me in many ways. Mostly though, I had learned over the past year that being at home in one's skin is the most important aspect of home. Sometimes we don't get to experience home as we'd like. But as long as we're at home in our own skin, we are truly home anywhere we travel.

One of Lisa and George's daughters, Lauren, had been teaching herself to surf all summer, and Lisa agreed to let Lauren be part of the photos (that appear on the web site *www.inspirebymichelle.com*); the idea was that I would interact with Lauren. However, as time drew closer, Pamela sent me an e-mail with a comment about both girls being in the photos. She said it would be about me watching them, as if I were watching a memory of Denise and me playing in the ocean.

Denise and I had played in the same waves along other parts of the Atlantic Ocean and on the Gulf Coast. But now I was taking the Lantz family board and paddling out past where the girls were playing. I was going to the "backside" of the waves to bring myself back to shore standing on a surfboard. The ocean was part of my past, my memories, but I was also creating new memories by venturing out into a different part of it. The picture would show me moving into the future as I surf, with water as a symbol of hope in my life, along with the happiness of my times in the water I had with Denise.

I am not leaving the past behind; it continues to weave through my current life. As Pamela and I discussed what outfits I should take to the beach that morning, all of them spread out on the bed of the guestroom of her house, she pointed to the bikinis and asked, "Which one would you have worn when you were younger?"

That was easy. I would have chosen the pink and orange one, not too far off the pink, green, and orange one I'd worn growing up in the years before I became too self-conscious to wear a bikini at all.

Without reading the book, the book that I hadn't finished writing or told her much about, she had gotten right to the heart of it: my return to the Michelle I had always been.

It was windy when we drove up to Rye; a hurricane hovered off the coast and was wreaking havoc with the winds and the tides. I wasn't sure if I was going to venture into the water on the board. Any surfers we saw out didn't stay in the water too long. It was breaking fast.

Still, we had photos to take, but when Pamela asked Lauren and Kristina to go out into the water (both wearing wet suits and me in my shorty wet suit) and play, Lauren said, "I don't play with her."

At first I was a little taken aback by the statement since we had been clear to them they would be playing in the water. Later, on the drive back to Salem, I realized that Lauren, whose long blond hair reminded me of my own, could have been me. The two sisters did play in the water that day, and Lisa said they often play together. But for most of my life, I probably would have said the same thing about Denise, that we didn't play together, even though we did. It was about my independence.

I did take the board into the water even though it was at least a foot shorter than my own board. It was hard to get past the breaks, though. They were coming fast, and I kept getting pounded. As rough as it looked from the shore though, it wasn't that bad. I wasn't scared. It wasn't overwhelming. It was just fast. I did try to get up several times and came close. Finally, I knew it was a losing battle, as I'd seen with the others out there earlier, and I bodysurfed back to shore.

I was happiest just to be out there. It felt like home.

EPILOGUE

Late September 2012

Where do I go from here?

There are many unknowns in my life right now. I often joke that while I have been open about many details of my life, I am keeping control of what I share with others.

I don't like the unknown. I like control, I have been a latecomer to learning the lesson of trusting and having faith. I've learned more about it in the past year than ever before, or maybe it's more that I've reached a deeper understanding of the lessons I've learned.

My article about sports and concussions made the front page of *The Naperville Sun* yesterday. A friend from junior high told me that they've enjoyed seeing my "smiling face" and reading my articles. My friend JJ and I saw our track coach, Marty Bee, who said he'd been reading my articles.

Twice in the past twenty-four hours I have heard "Harden My Heart" by Melissa Manchester on two different radio stations; the same song that Denise and I roller-skated around the basement to. Earlier this week, twenty minutes apart on the radio I heard my two very favorite songs from the 1980s, "St. Elmo's Fire" by John Parr and "Summer of '69" by Bryan Adams. I know that Denise was telling me she's with me as I continue to navigate this new road that is my old road. Perhaps it's the old road with new paving.

Whatever it is, I'm going forward on it. Sometimes I'll look back when I'm out running, wondering if someone is behind me and I think of the Manfred Mann lyric that you shouldn't look back because you've been there. But it's okay to look back because, yes, I was there, and being there has made me who I am.

And it's returned me to where I left off. Now it's time to pick up and make sure I accomplish everything I wanted then. I don't think of it as a second chance. Instead I see it as life truly taking me where I'm supposed to go. And I'm able to go in that direction because I took the time to walk the grief road and learn everything I was supposed to.

Now I can be the Michelle I always was and always wanted to be. I have a role to play for everyone although I never had any idea it was the role I played for myself: keeping myself motivated and inspired to be the best that I could be. I thought my writing would be about helping people escape their lives for a while and live in someone else's shoes, feeling that person's emotions and living that person's life. Although that may be part of my role, I see that mostly it's about inspiring people in the ways that I taught myself to keep hope alive.

When we are surfing, we instinctively look down. We look down at the board. What we really need to do is look ahead and see where we're going; straight out in front of us whether it's the hotels of Waikiki or the cliffs of Palos Verdes at Rat Beach. Both Sunny and Scott reminded me of this and each time they did, my success rate on the board jumped up a notch.

If we look back, we remember that we've been there and that's okay. But we still need to keep going, creating new memories. The future is where we're going. We're looking ahead of us, we're reflecting on what was, and we're enjoying the moment we're in.

Going forward on this new road doesn't mean I forget my sister. It's actually the opposite: it means I'm not forgetting who I am or who I'm supposed to be. That's the best way I can honor Denise and the life she lived. And I know she is happiest for me when I am being who I'm supposed to be.

www.ingramcontent.com/pod-product-compliance
Lightning Source LLC
Chambersburg PA
CBHW020903090426
42736CB00008B/481